Raped of Love

My Adoption Story

PRESTON JONES

authorHOUSE®

AuthorHouse™
1663 Liberty Drive
Bloomington, IN 47403
www.authorhouse.com
Phone: 1 (800) 839-8640

Published by AuthorHouse 09/25/2017

ISBN: 978-1-5462-0933-1 (sc)
ISBN: 978-1-5462-0931-7 (hc)
ISBN: 978-1-5462-0932-4 (e)

Library of Congress Control Number: 2017914458

Print information available on the last page.

This book is printed on acid-free paper.

Contents

You think you're where I want to be
your ego blinds you to see
I'm giving myself things you never gave me
being the person you said I'd never be
I found the love I need
I finally found me.

-Kiera Nicole

Introduction

THE PURPOSE OF this book is to bring you inside my mind and place you in my body and connect you to my feelings and memories as one entity. We will travel through my life and take my journey together. It is my hope that through my eyes you will perceive and feel all the emotions of my life's journey as if you were walking in my footsteps and living my memories as your own.

In all essence, you will feel and smell the very air that I felt and smelled. The purpose is for you to live my past, feel my present and think about our future... Remember we are one, you are looking through my eyes.

This book in no way has been written to assassinate anyone's character, that includes my father, my mother, or myself. This book is simply meant to give you the facts, exactly as they unfolded. These are not written to be judgmental but are, as stated before, the actual facts and feelings as they unfolded with the journey of my life. So please take a moment and clear your mind and forget civilization. Please take a journey in your mind with me and expand and feel your five senses, smell, sight, touch, taste, and hearing as you transform into me, Preston Jones. Please feel free to feel each emotion, cry when I cry and laugh when I laugh, come into my world. The gate keeper of secrets...this is my story.

Some names of the characters and locations in this book have been changed but all contents are as they actually happened.

Chapter 1

I, PRESTON JONES, was born October tenth nineteen sixty two at five thirty six in the morning in Westchester, New York. I spent the first eleven months of my life in foster care, and was later adopted by Theodore Roosevelt Jones, my dad, and Mildred Elizabeth Jones, my mom.

My dad was from Harlem, in New York City and stood six foot five and weighed in at two hundred and eighty five pounds. In his younger days my father was a Sunday School Teacher. Theodore, or Ted as his friends would call him, was a very intelligent man. He was a skilled carpenter, plumber, electrician, and disciplinarian. You will realize later in this book why I mentioned disciplinarian!

My mom, Mildred was born in Suffolk, Virginia. She was a very quiet but very humble lady. She always carried a public smile but she was also a keeper of secrets. My mom was about five feet three inches and one hundred and sixty five pounds. She had a mahogany complexion, was well proportioned, with a gorgeous head of hair. Mom was very witty and although she was quiet, she had a strong character. She never allowed you in her mind or personal space. She had very few people who were in her circle of friends, five people that I knew for sure.

We lived in a newly constructed house in a town called Greenburgh. Greenburgh was a town in Westchester, New York right outside of White Plains, New York. The house was a corner property that sat high up on a hill, Forty One Lincoln Place and South Road. All of the blocks were named after Presidents, Polk, Van Buren, Tyler, etc. There at Forty One Lincoln Place in the white house with the orange shutters resided myself, Preston, my brother Wilton, my mom Mildred, and my dad Theodore. There we were known as the Jones Family.

As a child about 3 years old I remember my mom being very sick in the bed. Through my mind, my mom looked to be in excruciating pain. I felt so hurt in my heart for her because she was in so much agony, my mom put on such a facade, she still possessed strength in her weakness. I knew she had to get better, I could not cook so I searched for something to get her that would give her enough strength, just to get out of that bed. All I could find was one peanut in the shell, so I brought that peanut to her and how her eyes lit up, it was like I had given her a full course meal, from soup to potatoes. My mom smiled, came to life, and said "Thank you, Pressy!" At that moment I knew what it was like to make someone happy and to have a warm heart. There my feelings as a caretaker started to evolve.

My brother Wilton was three years older than me so as an older brother he had some influence over me. He was supposed to be my example and strength but I always, for some reason, felt a distance from him. Wilton was what they called a hyperactive child. At that time he was always destructive and distracted. He was always getting himself into mischief and trouble. For example, Wilton would take my mom's lipstick with the top on it and then turn the lipstick so it would be all squished to the top leaving the lipstick unusable. He started fires in the house, hid the car keys so we were stuck at home, disconnect the telephones, empty mom's perfume bottles, the list goes on.

As you know, being the youngest child I would get blamed for the mishaps and my brother would some how convince me to take the blame for what mischief he had done and made me swear that I would not change the story or tell our parents the truth that it was Wilton who had done these things. And so began the secrets of the gatekeeper- a kind of dark superhero. This also began the start of creative yet intense beatings from my dad Theodore, The Disciplinarian.

My beatings started with switches from the Crab Apple tree in the backyard which I had to pick myself. Then I graduated to custom cut paddles to electrical extension cords, which in turn he made me rub alcohol on my open wounds after being beat. I guess the same beatings as the slaves received at times right?

After these beatings with the extension cords, there were extremely hot baths waiting for me to take. This was and had become the norm in my house for me. Along with my emotions diminishing, my endurance for the threshold of pain increased at least in my mind. I knew that all families must have these same discipline standards, but out of fear I kept my mouth shut. I became a stronger and better gatekeeper. My secrets and wounds were deeper and my walls were getting thicker.

Chapter 2

YEARS PROGRESSED AND so did my beatings which seemed to be coming more often, I would estimate pretty much weekly. I still have the faded marks from the extension cords on my inner thighs and left arm to this day. They serve as a reminder of what you might call a personal branding, branding me forever as a keeper of the gates, vowed to secrecy. So as these beating progressed and continued, it became to me a normal function of a family.

All my pain started to become internalized in my mind and introverted into my deepest thoughts and my emotions became null and void. In my mind this started the first seedlings of conflict from abnormal behaviors of love, care, and compassion. Yet, I knew what seemed to be normal in my family had to be suppressed in society and this all had to be held and locked up in my mind. I could never verbalize the pain with anyone because really this had to be my fault, otherwise, I would never had been beaten right?

As the years went by I still maintained a close relationship with my mom, for I was still a child looking for my mom's nurturing love. However, I still at that very young and tender age, could feel my thoughts and emotions for my brother and mother slowly start to diminish by the age of four or five. I started to alienate or isolate myself. First, it was mental preparation and then I would physically separate while in the midst of my family. For me I needed to function as the family did physically in body but in my mind and thought I was in another dimension, in my own Twilight Zone. So I began to learn to assimilate. In this process I still felt my mother's love but did not feel the same for my father and brother. The barrier of Plexiglas had started, invisible to all others but visible to me. To me it seemed as though, my father and brother were against me like the dynamic duo. Remember? Batman & Robin. My brother got me in trouble and my father administered the punishment.

Chapter 3

MY PARENTS WERE excellent providers for the family. There was no want materially. I remember so clearly one day around late Spring, early Summer in nineteen sixty seven, I was playing in the basement of our house, my mom came down stairs and pulled out a brown metal box and said, "Preston, if anything were to happen to your father or I, you are to find this box and open it."

My mother then showed me exactly where this metal box was hidden in the basement. This box had been hidden right there where I spent so much of my time. The basement was my world, my seclusion spot. That basement was my safe zone, my safe house, even though that was the designated spot for my beatings.

As days elapsed my curiosity got stronger and stronger as to what was in that brown metal box. The days turned into months, and finally the suspense had to be broken. I could no longer handle the anticipation of wonder, so I pulled out the box. I was about five and a half years old at the time. I slowly opened the box at the same time intently listening to see if anyone was coming down the stairs, which I could tell because the stairs had a creak in them. So while I intently listened for any creaking, I opened the box. All I saw was stacks of money, one hundred dollar bills, fifties and twenties. I would go through this money every day, it was my own dream and imaginary world. I would play with the money day after day, week after week always making sure that I placed it back in the box just as I had found it and putting the box back exactly where I had found it.

I did notice there were some other papers under the stacks of money. I knew the papers had to be placed back just a certain way because if it wasn't then I'd get the beating of my life. So far I was satisfied with all the money in front of me.

As time went on so did my curiosity. I wanted to know what were those papers that were taboo. So I removed the money and pulled the papers out and found two envelopes which of course I opened. This information was very confusing to me one envelope said Preston on it so I opened the envelope. I found a paper with a file number on it. Under the file number the content read:

'Let it be known that Rodney Snell, from this day forward shall be known as Preston Jones. Preston Jones born October 10th, 1962 at 5:36am at MT. Vernon Hospital.'

This totally confused me. I never celebrated birthdays because both my mom and dad were Jehovah's Witness, so I was already confused about the whole birthday thing. Being trained to learn to read and write from such a young age, by five I was advanced in my reading and writing skills and better comprehension than the average child my age.

---ₑᶜᵒ♥ᶜᵒₛ---

Chapter 4

O NCE I OPENED the first envelope (Rodney Snell) Then I opened the second envelope labelled Wilton Eric Jones. "Who's this?" I asked myself once again. Once again there was a file name on the envelope which said:

'John Lewis Thomas shall hereby known as Wilton Eric Jones, shall now be the legal child of Mildred Elizabeth Jones and born February 1960.'

Immediately my mind started desperately trying to put this Scooby Doo mystery together but I could not. In my mind, I asked myself, *'How could Wilton my brother be John Lewis Thomas? Most of all how could Rodney, Rodney Snell be Preston, Preston Jones? How could Rodney and*

Preston be the same person and have the same date of birth October tenth?' It just didn't add up day after day and month after month, I would hurry to go back down to the basement to look back over these papers and make sure I placed everything back just so. This got the best of me and ate me alive inside. Finally I had enough, I muscled up all my nerves to bring this preserved mystery up to my mother. I was filled with anxiety, confusion, and a quest for answers. I grabbed the two envelopes and marched up the seemingly endless flight of stairs which now in my mind seemed like an unending journey. I knocked on my mothers bedroom door, it was a hot day summer day. I could see the sweltering heat rise off the hot cement as I looked up at my mother who was blankly staring out at the hazy heat from her queen lounge chair facing the window. She looked as if she had been awaiting this moment in time for me to confront her.

My mom looks down at me, half turns with a stern but wondering face and looks deep in my eyes and said, "Yes Pressy, what do you want?" I looked at her, it felt as if I had enormous lumps in my throat larger than what I had imagined frog would have, then I looked at the two envelopes and looked at my mom. Her eyes widened a bit, she said, "What have you there, Pressy?"

I looked at the envelopes so as to think maybe this should be all over and I should just return these envelopes and act like this never happened. Of course I was past the point of no return. I took a deep breath not knowing how eternally this could and would forever alter my life as I had known life to be for approximately five and half years. I looked at the envelopes one more time and as I handed them to my mother I looked directly in her large brown eyes.

My mom looked down at me with what seemed to be an expected, most deep sadness that I had ever experience. There was more pain in her eyes than when I saw her sick in bed and brought her that one peanut in the shell in order to ease her pain. My mom looked at me and then looked at the two envelopes, she gently put the contents of one of the envelopes back into the envelope and sternly told me, "Put this envelope back into the box where you found it and we'll discuss this one."

So I did just that. I journeyed back down stairs and put the one envelope back in the box and made my way back upstairs which seemed to be an unending journey to my mother. Now looking in her eyes as she stared into the envelope's contents was a heavy deep hurt that seemed to far surpass the physical pain that I had seen my mother in before. The closest description was it seemed as if she had surpassed an emotional plateau of the deepest barrier of hurt humanly possible. Looking once again deep into my mother's eyes seemed as if her eyes were holding back a flood gate of surprise and hurt, a hurt straight from the heart. I guess looking back on this, this was the hurt of a broken heart, pushed back and covered by an invisible glass like glazed barrier, which in one blink would release the weakness of emotion of unbearable pain, tears!

Chapter 5

S O THERE I was looking at my mom as she desperately tried to hold back her emotions. Mom tried so hard not to blink, but that was humanly impossible. So now came the blink, one tear seemed to seep out followed by a series of single tears. Without uttering a word, she glanced at me and gently raised her hand and wiped the tears from her eyes, which now seemed to be never ending streams of emotions.

Mom then looked down at me and patted her lap, motioning me to sit on it, which I did. I put my head gently on her chest as if I were trying to listen to her heart and looked up at her face and that's when the words were spoken. Looking down a me through her swollen eyes she said, "Mommy loves you and I would go to the ends of this Earth before I give you up or let anyone try to take you from me! Do you understand me?"

"Yes mommy, I understand." I said. Then my mother paused. She looked at me and continued.

"Preston, Rodney is you! That was your name before you became my son, but all you need to know is I love you and always will and you are my son." She now lifted me off of her lap and wiped her tears off her face and as if by magic the tears stopped and all emotions changed as if this conversation never happened. Now looking at my mother's face, every past emotion had miraculously ceased like a plug in the bath tub full of water. There was not one trace of past flood emotions from just the few minutes previously. Now with a stern face my mom said, "Now Preston, go back down stairs and put this envelope back exactly the way you found it." (*Note: Please don't forget the second envelope, we will be discuss that later!)*

I was even more confused and devastated than before our conversation. But back then when your parents ended a conversation then that was it, no questions about it. Like I said I was even more confused and devastated and deeper in thought. I figured to myself, I should be playing with my Tonka trucks or Hot Wheel Cars, not dealing with this.

Well as you know by now, you have figured out that this is the beginning of being raped of love for me. Life had a whole new twist, my whole perception of what, in my mind of love was had changed totally. Inside, I drilled in my head that I could dare never to bring up this subject to my mom again. Looking at the pain I caused her, I could never mention this to anyone. So not only was I raped of love but started becoming a gatekeeper of secrets. Yet, I wondered *where is my mother? Who is my mother? What does my mother look like? Why would my mother give me away? Did she love me? What did I do wrong that made my mother not love me and give me away?*

I thought, '*So my mother is not my mother and my father is not my father and oh yeah, my brother Wilton is not my brother, then everything around me isn't real. In reality, guess what Preston? You are not Preston! Preston you are Rodney, Rodney Snell.*' I sat down in the basement and wept for what seemed like an eternity. It was the first time I felt alone and rejected. I knew that I had to still explore what was in the brown metal box. I needed more answers that I thought I could only find in that box. But that would have to be another day, right then that was way over my head and very overwhelming.

Later that evening, my dad came home I dreaded hearing the key go in the keyhole for I knew that would get the beating of a lifetime for violating and going into the box.

Chapter 6

AFTER MY DAD'S arrival home, I was trying to prepare myself for my beating. The minutes seemed to last hours and the hours into days as I awaited sore punishment. My dad took his shower, my mom made my favorite fried hot dogs and beans with molasses, brown sugar, onions, and toasted bread & butter. I could not enjoy it because who can enjoy a meal knowing they were to get the expected beating of a lifetime? Strangely enough, no beating! We had our regular daily bible study and then off to bed. Somehow I knew this was too good to be true. No whippings for going in the box?

Then came bedtime, my brother and I slept in the same room, I layed there in the dark listening to every footstep in the house. When my dad would come to the room and check on us my heart would jump because I figured he'd say, "Okay Preston, in the basement..." and that meant time for my beating. It never happened which I was happy but curious to why not? I got beat for everything else.

I was constantly waiting for the nights and days to come still expected that beating but it never happened. Many a days I wanted to tell my brother about my discovery and tell him about the envelopes but since it never came up, I never brought up the conversation with my brother about who he was or for the fact who he wasn't. I had already vowed that if I didn't get a beating for this then I would not mention it again. I did vow to myself that I would one day find my mother.

Once things cooled down in my mind, I continued my quest. Back to the box I went digging deeper and deeper and trying to memorize what information was on that paper like October 10th and that I was born at five thirty six in the morning, and that I was born at Mount Vernon Hospital. To my surprise besides those two papers there were no other clues to my past or for that my future. As my quest intensified I started looking thru the telephone book, looking for any Snell's in the Mount Vernon area. I would dial each and every Snell in alphabetical order. When someone would pick up the phone I'd ask "Are you missing a little boy? My name is Rodney Snell…"

Some folks would hang up, some would ask if I was lost and some would ask where my parents were. I would answer, "I don't know." and hang up. A few times I would be asked, "What is your mommy's name?" Of course I couldn't answer the question. A lot of people would just say sorry that they couldn't help. *(There wasn't any call waiting or caller I.D. then.)*

As years went by my curiosity got stronger and as I got older so did my levels of comprehension and reasoning as I stated before I was in training to be a minister since I could walk and talk. My parents were Jehovah's Witnesses, my father was an elder, so we still had daily readings of the bible and studied for my presentations. I was one of those young children knocking at your door early on Saturday mornings to place the Watchtower and Awake with you after my bible presentation. How glad I am to have had that valuable training and rigorous study habits little did I know how much it would help me later on in life with my search for my mom.

Once again I anxiously started to imagine how my mom looked and how tall she was and if I had any brothers or sisters. I often wondered where my place or role was in life even though I was in the Jones house, I felt as if I didn't belong. Again and again, I would go through different papers in that box thinking that somehow I had missed something.

My thread of thinking was erratically changing when my dad would taste test our cereal in the morning and put his spoon back in the pot it repulsed me to the point of not eating. When asked why I didn't want to eat all I could say is that is was nasty to lick or put the spoon back inside I felt this is not my father and he is putting his germs back in the pot. This only lasted a while and then my dad would make sure he rinsed the spoon off after he tested our food.

In the morning before we left for school we would give our mom and dad a kiss and hug, everyday before we left the house. Yes I would always hug and kiss them and say have a good day but I also reserved a third of that hug or kiss for my mother, I knew one day I would be able to give her my portion of love. (I know this all sounds a bit strange to you but these are the facts.)

At night when we would say our good night prayers and hug our parents good night when I got in the bed I would imagine giving my mom her good night hug and kiss also. Each night brought in that lonely feeling of wanting and yearning for my mom. I was convinced that one day I would find my mom, in reality my search had just begun.

Interestingly, there was a scripture that always kept in my mind as a child that I loved it was Proverbs 5:1-3, which says

"My son pay attention to my wisdom, listen carefully to discernment, so that you may guard your thinking abilities and safeguard knowledge with your lips."

From there I learned to pay attention and listen carefully and guard what I was thinking and keep what knowledge I had to myself and from then keep my mouth shut.

---ᐧⱺ♥ⱺᐧ---

Chapter 7

School

LIFE WAS PRETTY much the same day to day simply going to school, riding bikes, studies, playing ball and going to the park. My parents started going on a lot of weekend getaways and also sometimes had conflicting work schedules so my parents got us a babysitter, her name was Debbie. There was a young lady who was one of our care takers.

I remember when I was young when my parents left she would tell me to take off my clothes and she would play with play with my penis and make lay me lay down with her. She would tell me to give her a needle; I guess she called herself trying to have sex with me."

Once again I kept this a secret and this happened time and time again year after year. In my mind at that time this was not such a bad thing being a boy and all, As children we all played house and would experiment and kiss and touch each other but that was with children your own age. In reality, I was a child and Debbie was an adult. As years went on I guess Debbie moved away or went on to another college. I never saw her again.

Going through Elementary School and Middle school I stayed close to my friend Dondi, who lived on the other side of town. He lived in the projects on Manhattan Avenue and I lived in the suburbs. Nevertheless, Dondi was a Jehovah's Witness also, just like myself. Dondi didn't celebrate birthdays or Halloween which we knew was Hollow's Eve- or the day of Satan the Devil. Of course we didn't celebrate Christmas we knew that December 25th was not the birthdate of Jesus and the two holidays were coincided in order to keep the Christians and the Pagans in unity. The worship of the God of the Sun for the Pagan believers and for the Christians the worship of the Son of God, Jesus, which today has been proven by theological professors. So Dondi and I bonded since we were the only two well known Jehovah's Witnesses that stood up for our principles in the entire school.

When the class celebrated these holidays, we stuck together and this kept a large stress off me being the lone wolf and I took a lot of stress off of Dondi having to stand up by himself. So when the class celebrated these holidays we would sit outside the class in the hallway or go to the library or gym until the festivities were over.

Dondi, or Diego as I would call him seemed to be very strong and mentally mature to me and very sure of himself. Yet he was a soft spoken, very humble, person. Dondi and his brothers were all known for their natural athletic abilities. It ran in his family. Anything he joined in athletically, Dondi excelled. Come to think of it was no big deal to Dondi because it was natural. He had such a mild mannerism about him that really drew me close to him. I noticed he was a very good listener. When you talked to Dondi, he would just look at you and listen a lot of the times. That's all he did was listen and not respond or he would just say 'I hear ya!'

Many days in elementary school (O.T.R.) Dondi and I would sit on the wall at lunch time and talk. Dondi was the first person that I ever tried to expose my secret identity to.

One warm day while sitting on the wall, Dondi was tapping with his pencils on the cement (he loved playing the drums and had a crazy habit of chewing on plastic straws.) Any how, while we were sitting on the wall and Dondi was playing his imaginary drum set when I said, "Dondi."

"What's up, man?" He said.

"Do you want to know my real name?" I said. Dondi of course said.

"Bro, I already know your name it's Preston, Preston Jones!"

I for some reason got so intensely upset with Dondi as if I expected him to know my secret identity somehow. Well I raised my voice and said, "No my name is NOT Preston, it's Rodney, Rodney Snell!" Dondi looked over at me with disbelief and at first didn't utter a word he played another beat and looked at me and said. "Stop tripping bro, stop tripping."

So I knew he didn't believe me or comprehend what I was trying to tell him or the urgency. So I stuffed everything back into my inner soul and pushed back my secret and never exposed or shared that thought again with Dondi or with anyone else for that matter.

As years went by Dondi and I stayed close and we were tight friends even through the early years of High School. Dondi's world was a bit different, he started playing high school sports, track, basketball, and as I said before Dondi was naturally athletic so he excelled and I believe he was even the captain of the basketball team. So even though we always recognized each other our paths separated. We were on two different journeys. Dondi was pursuing his dreams as Dondi could and should. And I was still lost and confused and trying to put a solid foot on my journey. The journey to find out who I was and who Rodney Snell was and who was my mom and family? I was in my adolescent years.

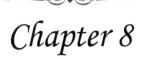

Chapter 8

Adolescent Years

OUR HIGH SCHOOL started in the 7th grade. Life changed a bit for me. My father purchased a brownstone building in White Plains, NY on Ferris Avenue. We worked and converted the ground floor which was a beauty shop into a candy shoppe called 'Sweet Tooth.' My father did all the electrical conversions, masonry, and carpentry work. The store was geared as an old fashion candy store with the large jars of candy on the shelves which children could get a wide variety of penny candy. You might remember some of them, Sixlets, Dots, Mary Jane's, Coconut Strips, Bazooka gum, candy fish and so many varieties of chocolate penny candies.

We would go to Hershey, Pennsylvania once a month and stock up on all our candy. That was the chocolate capital of the United States then. So now once Sweet Tooth Candy Shoppe was established, then the responsibility of setting up and opening the store became mine. By then my brother, Wilton had been sent away to different group homes for boys years prior, so it was just me. So everyday after school I would get on my bike and ride to the shoppe to set up before my dad got off his job. (Which he was now employed as radiologist.) I would sanitize the ice cream machine, light the grills, put water in the hot dog bun steamer, turn the oil on for the fryers for the Chicken and French fries. Sometimes I would sell the neighborhood children candy or cookies from the store until my dad and my mom came in and the store was in full effect. I then became a familiar face in the neighborhood and got to know all the drug dealers and street hustlers, number writers,(bookies) mothers and fathers, children by name from the neighborhood, including my first run in with the Mafia there.

I met my next soon to be best friend then who lived straight down the block on Ferris Avenue. All in White Plains knew him by the name Big Tim or Squeeze. Tim was my age and where I stood about five foot six inches then, Tim was every bit of six feet 3inches at the least. Tim was a big fella and always laughed and had a giant sense of humor. Tim was a happy go lucky type of individual and from me getting to know the people on the block, I got to learn that Tim was an entrepreneurial type of person in which I was also, being that I pretty much ran The Sweet Tooth and would go to the Candy Distributor weekly to get supplies for the store, therefore I learned how the operation of getting the candy cheap and in bulk allowed you to sell at lower cost making a profit for what you sold sometimes a hundred percent profit. Then all else it was a no brainer. It was time for me to try to start my own business in school.

Tuesdays I would get my supplies, cookies and candy, and on Wednesdays, I would dress up in all green, green shirt, pants, and green puma sneakers. I would sell my product at a lower rate than the candy and vending machines the school had setup. I would stand in front of those vending machines and sell my own product and also when I was in class I was known as Hustle man. So while the seniors were selling weed I would sell the munchies. So together we had an understanding.

Then I started thinking, '*hey I know all these people now, perhaps I could establish a one stop shop?*' So I upgraded, I started selling beer cold in the summer, I would get them as close to frozen as possible, then wrap them in aluminum foil to keep them cold all day. Now the seniors didn't have to cut school to get beer, I had it at a good price and was in high demand to a select crowd of people. So I was using my entrepreneurial skills at school on Wednesdays and running the family store the rest of the week.

That's where Tim came in or should I say Big Tim. He was a hustler and I was a hustler. When it snowed we shoveled snow and when fall time came we raked leaves. We had our hands in whatever made money and of course some things I can't discuss but use your imagination. So Tim and myself both loved to hustle and so down to the infamous 42nd street or the deuce as we would call it. Down to 42nd street we went in the Big Apple, Manhattan, New York City, NY. To the hustle street itself. You could find everything on 42nd street from prostitutes to watches. Like we would say from hoes to Hollywood.

Chapter 9

Hustle Years

S O THERE WE were, we figured that Christmas time would be our big hustle. I got a shipment of Perfume from a Factory in Tuckahoe, NY. Next stop was Grand Central Station. We peddled in the Christmas spirit up and down the escalators we rode and yelled our *'Perfumes. Perfume here get your perfumes! Make your wife and girlfriends happy for Christmas! 3 for $25 get them while they last!'* With the perfume came a nice black velvet box. We did good for about four hours, it was truly the Holiday spirit and people were buying. We made our way out to the street, it was a crowded hustle and bustle, people buying hotdogs and jewelry, and snow was falling. The streets were packed you could smell the aroma in the air of the street Vendors hot pretzels. The air was crisp and cold but clear you also smell the distinct aroma of chestnuts being sold from an open fire. There were plenty of smiles and good spirit and crowds of people stopping at the stands of the vendors as they yelled out whatever product they were vending or whatever product they were hustling. All you could hear was:

"Hotdogs here! Get your hotdogs, mustard, sauerkraut, chili!!! Hot pretzels, hot pretzels here! Get 'em while they're hot!"

"Fresh chestnuts, fresh chestnuts!"

"Get your watches here ten dollars, ten dollars! Get your Seiko watches here!"

Then you look up and see the Neon color signs that have an arrow pointing upstairs flashing on and off in a variety of colors that said

'Girls, Girls, Girls' and then you hear *'Girls, girls, girls, check 'em out upstairs twenty dollars for an half hour! Girls, Girls, Girls, take a look, check em out!"*

As the snow fell and the snow built up on the sidewalks it seemed more people came out. This was hustle heaven. Christmas lights and neon billboards lit up this area and Christmas carols played through the street speakers the store fronts had Christmas decorationsin the windows some had machanical moving train displays some had movig nativity seens, there were plenty of familys shopping in the Christmas spirt trying to find last minute Christmas deals everyone seemed to be in a happy festive spirit, as the evening approached and daylight turned to night so to the city became even more vibrant there were now neon lights everywhere even some of the sky scrapers were totally adorned in lights seemed as though on each corner peddlers were selling Christmas trees and Christmas ornaments, as snow built up on the side walks so did the crowds of people and so did the huslers and peddlers and vendors, there we joined in amongst the other vendors. 'Get your hotdogs here and Hot pretzels' and 'Girl, Girls, Girls' came and checked us out: *"Perfumes three for twenty five dollars!"* We fit right in and started our hustle and drawing a crowd.

Next to us was a street hustler, who had a cardboard box with three folded playing card two black spades and one red hearts he set up his table in seconds and yelled, *"Check it out, find the red card and make fifty dollars! Check it out!"* He would switch and mix the cards, then tell you to point out the red card but put twenty dollars down if you picked out the red card after it was scrambled you'd get fifty dollars. One out of ten people might win. Then he'd move on to the next corner. It was called three card molly.

Oh, we loved this new found life of hard, fast, quick hustle and we were good at it. I fell in love with this street hustle quick money and big money. A white gentlemen walked up to us and asked us "How much for everything?" We looked at each other figured three hundred.

"Three hundred and we walk away. You get everything."

He said, "I'll take it!" We thought we had made it to the big hustle, until the man pulled out his badge. He was the peddler police, he was five-O. So he confiscated all of our products. We still had a few hundred in our pockets, so we were okay. I loved the exhilaration of the hustle and Hollywood at the time. It was demand and needs, I thought if I had what was in demand then I could get what I needed and so now I was about to enter the mouth of the dragon not only did I love the hustle but I started getting high.

Chapter 10

Hustle High, Get High

AS I CONTINUED my newfound love of hustling, I would have a beer now and then. I noticed that drinking beer seemed to take the edge off my inner stress, as well as open a different kind of social world. I often noticed that when I drank with the fellas, that any and all conversations that came were a hundred percent acceptable. When doing business or hustling on the streets the drinking of alcohol seemed to open my mind of self thought to a slightly different dimension.

My thoughts of my mother and finding her now intensified as I progressed in my years of life. I functioned in society only to survive but not primarily to live. Even though now there was a constant supply of people who chose to be around me I would limit their company and only chose to keep a select few in my inner circle. For a while I transitioned to upstate New York, in Pleasantville. I turned sixteen and I was on my own. A Cottage School is where I became employed and ironically this was a group home for kids whose parents gave their children up or children whose parents were street characters. You know pimps, prostitutes, addicts, and pushers. Most of the kids were there because their parents just didn't care about them and some because they just did not care or respect their parents. Every kid there, though, was from New York City. There, at the time I was introduced to weed or what they called reefer.

Weed to me seemed to be the great mind expander and as you already know I was already always deep in thought, trying to find my own identity. Smoking weed would intensify my thoughts. Now my thoughts allowed me to contain and journey into my own head into my own thoughts and I now became in unison and I became my own thoughts like looking down at myself from the outside distance and looking deep inside. At times I would see the world and people as if I were a hawk soaring high above and looking down having the ability to swoop down into my own head and pull out whatever was negative and drop that thought out of existence. Like the Native Americans I felt one with the world, one with nature. My mind pushed to the outer limits and my imagination out witted the best of all fantasies. Because in my mind all fantasies became reality. Life was a never ending vertex to infinity and infinite thoughts were powers of solutions. I finally became one with the universe and at peace even with the ramblings of my own mind.

I was for the first time able to be outside myself while living in my own body. It seemed that when I got high that inner strength of my deepest core was expanded to new dimensions. I no longer had to sleep to dream, I was wide awake and not only could I dream but I would fantasize and now the world became my playground and the universe, my Disney World futuristic, scientific, adventurous, frontier and fantasy, all in one at my minds disposal. All the above was an escape from my pain, hurt, and frustration in which when I came down from the high, I was still alone in a city of millions still through all this chaos and confusion I still kept good jobs. I now found myself becoming more of a nomad moving from city to city. Now I started hustling cocaine powder which drew around me a totally different classification of characters called white collar workers. These were higher clientele of individuals but now I had to balance my actions and thoughts to those I was catering to and of course my suppliers which were Italians and of course Dominicans. You might be familiar with the names Mafia or Cartel in which I had daily dealing with.

I knew to keep my mouth shut to what I knew, seen, and heard. I was all business and of course had been very adept in keeping things a secret since the age of five. Because that's what I was the keeper of secrets, the gate keeper. So I was a natural. Now I set up shop in the Big Apple, once again my hustle was on. I sold to some big wigs, some of my clients were CEO's of corporations, executives, corporate managers, top dogs, of fortune 500 companies. Top CEO's of financial institutions. With this distribution came certain privileges and certain power. Just like any other business it's who you rub shoulders with it's not what you know but who you know.

I also had some things to hold over these clients heads so it was that I had to trust that they would not blow the whistle on me. They had to trust that I wouldn't blow the whistle on them. They had to trust that I would supply and I met their demands and in turn those who supplied me kept one eye on me because with one mistake or slip of the tongue my very existence would cease to exist forever. So now I had to become the Master Gatekeeper of Secrets times three. I remember one of my deeper connections telling me:

"You know what the secret to the trade that you have taken up is?"

- **You never rat out your partner.**
- **You never mention your partner's name.**
- **You never use your product.**

"These are your golden rules. You follows these and you might and I say might live to be successful. But for sure if you violate number two and mention my name you will never live to tell this story. So now you figure out the rest. Now as for number three never use your own product…" That didn't work for me. As time went on I started wondering what was it about this drug cocaine that keeps these influential people coming back and risking it all just to get high? Sometimes I would watch them spread, sniff, and snort the powder cocaine. My perception was soon as the individual or client took a good sniff or snort I would see their eyes widen and seemed as if they had hit second gear or hit another dimension or went into warp drive as in Star Trek. They would sit up straight as if they were in the thrill ride of a lifetime, some would act as if they had seen God himself in all his glory and had announced them with the ultimate power and confidence of Jesus Christ. I would watch this time after time and from what I heard sex was even intensified times ten when you took coke. Hell, it seemed euphoric even the movie stars were snorting coke.

Chapter 11

White Line Blew My Mind

NEEDLESS TO SAY, once again curiosity got the best of me. I remember clear as day while living in Brooklyn, East New York. A young lady who was in my company asking me, "You ever try this?" referring to cocaine. I empathetically said no!! She looked at me, snorted another line and said, "Really, this is the stuff that make me Superman fly! You're crazy Pres! This is what Superman's cape is made of!"

I looked at her for a fleeting moment to ponder on her words then I commented back to her and said, "You're crazy this is straight kryptonite!" all the while doubting my own words to her. She blew another line looked at me and said, "Think about it all the people in high places and famous people are putting this up their noses. Lawyers, movie stars, and wall street dudes!" I knew she was right and had a point. She took another line, I watched her and thought about rule number three: **Never use your product.** Once again curiosity got the best of me so there I went chopped it, spread it with the razor in three lines and *snort, snort*. Three lines with a pointed straw my nostrils stung for a minute and she handed me a glass of water and told me to put my fingers in the glass and sniff a few drops of water behind the hits like you would a chaser for a shot of whiskey and so I did.

As the water dripped down my nostrils to the back of my throat my nostrils became crystal clear. Seemed like I was getting pure oxygen. My capillaries in my brain opened up as my eyes widened like quarters. Everything seemed so crisp and clear like breathing air on a winter day.

Even my hearing had increased I felt as if I could hear the cars coming from my way down 2 or 3 city blocks I could hear all the secrets of the city I could hear people's whispers magnified it seemed as if I were floating on a rainbow cloud of tranquility and I was sitting on the throne of God. Oh my God, I was invincible totally supreme and felt I had the philosophies of Einstein at my disposal at the same time I felt an euphoric burst of energy like I never had felt before I was Leonardo da Vinci had found the fountain of youth.

I felt the power of an Egyptian Pharaoh riding a chariot pulled by the fastest Arabian stallions as my body tingled, I could feel the blood flow and rush through my veins. My sexual stimulation seemed unbearable. I felt like a wild bull in heat, I felt as if i were the anointed one, the predictor of the world Nostradamus. I felt lighter than air! Oh my God, I was in love! I was in love with this feeling, I was in love with this high. I was at the peak of me.

I was about to burst with power, might, and in theory I felt uncontainable but yet satisfied. I felt as if I were the magnet and the world attracted and stuck to me. I felt the exhilaration of connecting with my body's most inner room, my heart. How good this was, the eraser to my pains. It was the eraser to my fear of finding who Rodney really was. Hell, it was the eraser of me the person I had known my whole life and I wanted to stay right there at that moment forever and a day.

I had never and I mean never had felt so alive and more vibrant. The trap was strong and I was caught and so now came the chase. I began chasing that moment and that high. I began chasing that moment. From that moment I started chasing, I started losing. I was now the hamster on the wheel in a glass cage- open and exposed. Still through this my thirst to find my mother could not be quenched. It became unbearable. I knew I could not possibly continue to function everyday life like this. Not Monday thru Friday. I still had a business to run and so I still hustled but became a weekend warrior. Now came the club scene.

Music became a big part in my use of cocaine. Getting high and going to the clubs went hand and hand. Cocaine, clubs, and lights were the era. I would go to the clubs listen to music, make my money, but at the same time I noticed that when I was in the clubs high, this whole music concept took on a different power. It seemed as if I could travel in between the beats and I could feel the rhythm in my soul. Once again I allowed myself to be one with the music. I became engrossed in the music as would the composer of a masterpiece. I became one with the beats as if I was an African tribal dancer. It seemed as if the combination of music and cocaine brought me to a spiritual climax and almost became erotic to my mind, sensual.

This you may or may not understand but if you don't I am attempting to bring you inside the experience. This was the Disco Era the eightys to late ninetys. I began to decipher the different acoustic instrumental when listening to drums, trumpets, sax, flute, bongos, the bass, treble and midrange. All different entities but yet they served an harmonious purpose to make music to catch your ear.

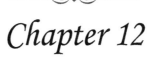

Chapter 12

Climax

A T THIS POINT I had become fully engulfed in the fantasy world of getting high. I transition from weekend warrior to being on the front line. I lived to get high and got high to live. Not even the thought of a woman overpowered my desire to get high. Like it is said on the street: Cocaine is the girl, heroine is the boy. So I began to have a deep intimate love affair with cocaine (the girl.) powder fish scales. I started thinking how deep and erotic it would be to have this feeling of being a warrior an invincible warrior and to climax or a have an orgasm at the same time. I felt this would be the highs of all highs. I thought to infinity and beyond and so I did and so it was, the ultimate mind and body pleasure. So now I was trapped I was running on the hamster wheel. I was killing myself while I thought I was outsmarting the world. I turned myself into a self contained guinea pig. I was the experiment, I was beating myself up so hard I actually thought I was winning. So I kept selling to get high,

By now I was working for a well Corporation in Manhattan, NY, as a manager. That was in corporate management. I thrived and worked in various locations from 51st and Broadway to 47-50 Rockefeller Center. There where I worked I also hustled cocaine to lawyers and CEO's of large firms. I supplied their demands. They didn't have to hit the streets for what they needed. I was just a phone call away, like a delivery service from a Chinese restaurant. I was a one stop shop.

My empire was well established but psychologically my life was a disaster. I was an abandoned building from the Bronx, physically standing but empty and cold inside. I had the human structure but a cold draft constantly blew through my soul, I put on such a facade of strength that all who were in my circle knew of my positivness but inside I was no more than a lifeless corps walking I had been on a mission to chase a high for years which I could never reach the original intensity. I was chasing a dream. So now my soul was dark, lonely, miserable, and thirsty and cold. I never forgot my quest to find my mother but for now it was pushed so far back that it seemed that it was out of reach. Now my arms were too short to reach my own dreams of finding my mother. My mind had become so murky and cloudy and disillusioned, that I constantly became caught in my own thoughts of self satisfaction.

I knew I was caught in a deep trap, caught in the web. The more I tried to get out the deeper I got. The more I tried to wiggle out, the more tangled I became. The ice was now too thin and I had fallen despite all the warning signs posted. Many times I would get lost in my own thought wondering how much simpler life could have been if I had never opened that box in the basement. Many days I would look at my birth certificate with my name Rodney Snell on it take another sniff of cocaine, numb the pain, and continue on that mission. All at the same time of being my own cheerleader cheering a team whom had already lost their spirit that team was myself but for the sake of the on lookers I kept a strong and loud agressive cheer for myself. Deep down I knew I was in the battle of my life. I was in the battle from keeping myself from losing my whole mind and life revolved around cocaine.

White line had blown my mind. I was caught, I was trapped by the same trap I had set for others. What would I do? How could I escape? It certainly wasn't by taking another hit was it? I started thinking back on principles that I was brought up on trying to find the good in the pain of my past. I would isolate myself, self diagnosing I tried the only means I knew.

Correction, I started going back to the Kingdom Hall of Jehovah's Witnesses on Sundays in Brooklyn. This lasted for a while and I began to see the light but some how in my perverted cloudy thoughts, I missed my misery. I seemed to miss my slavery to cocaine and of course my misery was refunded, I went back to the devil. Jehovah didn't leave me, I left Jehovah. For Jehovah God never leaves us we leave him and so the gates of hell were opened and the devil stretched his arms out and embraced me and chuckled for he knew I was a born child of God but searched to the devil and addiction to find comfort and love. The devil held me and hugged me right down to the ground floor of hell and so now the doors open.

Chapter 13

A ND SO WELCOME to hell. Crack cocaine, a dark, lonely, uncaring, self centered, without shame world of addiction. I learned as the higher class of people then called it "How to free base," that is smoking cocaine in it's purest form. There were many ways of cooking cocaine. Simply put three parts cocaine, one part baking soda, add a small amount of water in a test tube or Pyrex cooking jar, use a butane torch or light, heat the product some, and put ice in it to cool it down. The product turns to oil then crystallizes into a hard rock. Break it into smokable pieces and then smoke the rock out of a glass stem with a screen or bong. I even starting cooking the base(crack in the microwave)

Your watch the smoke twirl as you inhale which seems to be a hypnotizing effect as the cloud which you're watching enters your body you will feel your body transform like you were being possessed by evil spirits. Then the blast instantaneously leaving a emptiness in your soul. The addiction crack cocaine is very psychological and intense. Somehow it always gives you the illusion that you're strong enough to quit anytime you wanted as you get deeper and deeper into the addiction. Smoking crack is like a magician hypnotizing you and telling you to act or bark like a dog at the end of your hypnotzing session you would look back and not believe what you had done just for the high.

In the high of smoking crack it creates so many illusions in your mind and paranoia and self awareness. I remember sitting at an a friend's house in Brooklyn, Parkside Ave. My friend, was hitting the pipe. I was sniffing coke but he was smoking he took a hit and became paranoid. He looked over at me and motioned me to be quiet. "*Shhh...* Put everything away!" My friend crept over to the door and peeped out the peep hole, looking as if someone was on the other side. He then backed down on his knees, looked under the crack of the door to see if there were any shadows under the door.

He then held the doorknob to keep it from what he thought was turning then he put his ear to the door, "*Shh shh*, you hear them?" he said, "I hear walkie talkies, that's the Police!"

At other times he would put rice krispies or cornflakes under the door or doormat so he could hear if anyone was standing by his door or so he could hear anyone approaching his door. Sometimes he'd put a penny on the doorknob so if anybody tried to turn his doorknob he'd see the penny fall. To me at the time this was very comical who knew that one day I would be the star of the show. I'd be doing the same and worst. To make things short I tried a hit or a blast nothing happened. I thought, *'What a waste.'* I tried a second time and nothing. I tried a third time I took what they called a master blaster and *BAM*! There it was, I felt the most highest purified high I ever had. This had indeed far surpassed the days of insanity and hell began. Crack cocaine increased my insanity and stripped my mind of everything that was normal including my sleep pattern. I became a zombie. I lost my normal functions as a human being. I defied logic.

Chapter 14

Life Altering Changes

MY CHOICE OF drugs was about to change once again. I had a new hustle selling crack cocaine at the same time I would dabble and smoke on the weekends. I was what you would might call a weekend warrior. We opened a spot up in Brooklyn, I saw many people's life change through a peephole. I watched through the peephole as some people who just came on Friday night or Saturday, to people that came everyday and some of the people that you might see once a week started coming daily. So through this peephole I was able to see people change from recreational users to full blown addicts. We sold a wide variety from twenty dollar pieces to (big eight) eight balls, and weight.(cookies)

This was a simple process the customer would knock on the door, I'd ask what you need. They would state what they wanted I'd wait until they put the money thru the hole first. Then I'd hand the product to them thru the hole in the door or under the door. The people I had the most contact with were the street girls or hookers as we would call them. These girls would come everyday four or five times a day, weekends included. They took no time off, they were also called crackheads or chicken heads. I have seen many people sell their souls for crack, for just one hit. I remember on many occasions seeing ladies doing unimaginable acts just for a hit of crack.

I had learned so much through personal experience and gained plenty of knowledge about the streets and how the game was played in the streets. I believe I received my degree in streetology. I didn't go to

Harvard, I went to the University of Streetology. I even got my degrees as a Chemist. There were certain formulas and cuts used to break down and cut purity of every drug. I also learned the terminology of drugs for example 'Chasing the Dragon' was cooking cocaine and dope together and smoking them together. The 'Genie' crack mixed in with your cigarette. 'Whollie' was a cigar with weed laced with crack cocaine. 'A Blast' or 'Beam me up Scotty' was smoking crack thru a glass pipe. 'Speed ball' was shooting coke and dope thru your vein also called a 'Mainline'

Not going or shooting heroin straight in your vein but just under the skin was called 'Skin Popping'. 'Smoking embalming fluid in leaves was called 'Dusted' or 'Leaky Wet'. Powder cocaine called the 'Girl, Fish scale or whiteline.' and so on and so forth. Different brands of weed names: Exotic, Chronic, Ganga, Home, Red, Skunk, Camel Hair, Tye, Green etc. Sniffing dope or heroin was called: K-9, Mad Dog, China Girl, Boy. Crack cocaine was: Crack, base, mindbender and of course 'The Fire' because no matter how you use crack cocaine you always got a burnt in the end.

I say all of this to let you know that I was well educated on the streets and had seen all the warning signs of addiction and had experienced many versions of addiction. Personally saw how low and how fast peoples life deteriorated in the crack world and still I once again started using my own product and this time proved almost suicidal. This drug took more out of me psychologically than physically. My sleep patterns changed, my eating patterns changed and my thinking changed.

Once I was in the full grips of crack cocaine it sucked the life out of me from the inside out. Let me explain. My whole world was surrounded with what did I needed to do to get high? Getting high was my priority, getting high was my full time job, Sunday to Sunday, twenty four hours, plus overtime. Eating, bathing, sleeping, were secondary functions in my life. I did whatever I had to do in order to hear that rock sizzle in my pipe and to get high. I had self enslaved myself to cocaine. Crack cocaine my soul was sold.

After taking a hit of crack and there was no more there was a stage that we in the drug world was called 'Geeking.' No matter how hard you tried or where you were your eyes became glued to the ground looking for a piece of crack that somehow you thought you dropped, hoping you'd find a piece so you could continue your high. Sometimes the Geeking would last hours. This was a complete altering of you mind this would never happen on a normal day but now this was everyday so it had become my normal. There was nothing that I would not steal or no one that I would not deceive. No one I would not hurt physically or mentally for my addiction. There are no friends in the drug world or street games. You might have associates but once again I repeat there are no friends in that world.

There was nothing sacred to me, church, family, neighbors, or police. There are no fences or boundaries that surpassed my need for getting high all my normal thinking abilities were null and void. There were days that I stayed awake with no sleep the longest stretch I could remember was four days that twenty four hours times four. You don't stop until your body drops, simple. The average person smoking crack will go days without eating, drinking water, or bathing. Hot summer or dead cold winter or freezing cold rain does not hinder a crack head from getting high at least it didn't hinder me. I saw many delusions and illusions while being up for days smoking. The best way to explain to you is I saw mirages like a thirsty person being beat down with the heat of the desert seeing a lake of water in the distance.

I was sitting on my porch one hot day, I was drinking Old English Eight Hundred(OLD JESUS) and had been smoking for two days straight. I looked down the block and the whole block transformed into the Wild Wild West, let me explain. The roads were cobble stone, there were people riding horse drawn buggies. I saw and could hear the hooves of the horses coming down the street. People were doing their daily duties, going to the markets, saloon, ladies walking around with their umbrellas. I could even smell the horses I went back upstairs and came back down after taking another blast and nothing changed. The block was still transformed to the same scene to this day I have no explanation but I know what my eyes saw. There was a period of time that when I got high in my house I'd get so paranoid that I would see shadows of people behind my doors in my house and saw shadows behind my shower curtain which of course I would take a butcher knife and stab thru the curtain, leaving holes in the curtain. To this day I wondered was that all in my mind or was I leaving myself open to demonic influences. What was I seeing? Or was there some vortex or a gateway to Satan's world when I smoked crack?

What if there would have been actual people there? I surely would have injured or killed them if they were hiding behind that curtain. Imagine how unsafe of an atmosphere it was to others. Me getting high and grabbing a butcher knife like an idiot but then again people I got high with did these things and I was not the only one that had seen transform like I did. This was normal in that world. Now I think how insane that was. Insanity but yet that's what I was insane. Insane in the membrane. This all just a tip of the iceberg. Day after day, year after year. I stayed and lived as a warrior in this vicious cycle. I felt deplete, discouraged but not embarrassed or ashamed for I was on a mission to stop my pain. A mission to escape myself. My insanity had become a normal part of everyday life for Preston Jones, but not for Rodney. Not for Rodney Snell, Rodney Snell wanted to find his roots and his connections. I thought to myself, *'Preston, you got to get off this hamster wheel. In order for you to start your journey.'* Or I would be forever lost in my own web. I would be forever burning in my own torment of self induced hell. Preston had gotten sick and tired of getting sick and tired. Preston was tired of Preston.

It was time to find out who exactly was Rodney, who is Rodney Snell and where were you mommy? Where were you? Now my journey was to get myself together to get clean from addiction so after numerous attempts and years and at least fifteen detoxes, many rehabilitation centers from New York City to Upstate NewYork. Of course being a regular guest in jail and shelters and being homeless. The smoke started to clear and so too I thought my thinking progress had began to clear.

Chapter 15

Homeless

B EING HOMELESS WAS about the most spiritual intervention that I had in my life. It was raw pain and lonely thoughts cold streets and cold people. It was pure survival. Survival was myself and my thoughts accompanied with a card board box to lay on the ground to create what ever barrier that I could from the frozen cement street that I would lay my head on in the night. I remember my turning point was one bitter cold night in Manhattan, New Year's Eve to be exact. I was walking down 42nd street hungry, cold and lonely and as Time Square was filling up with thousand of people happy, drinking, young couples and old couples all happy and celebrating with horns, confetti, carrying champagne and wine. The snow was falling as I watched them as they were bringing in the New Year with wishes of happiness and promises of New Year resolutions of success. Here I was empty and cold and felt useless and without hope I was destitute. I was stripped of me, I had reached rock bottom, any lower and that would have been 6 feet under which at that moment did not seem to be the worst of ideas. Once again the weather was bitter cold my finger tips had no feelings and my toes felt as if they had been amputated I no longer had feeling in them, the wind was whipping around the corner at such a great magnitude of velocity that it was pushing me back against my forward motion as the snow swirled around me and the wind pushed me back from any forward movement and the wind started to howl as if the wind had a voice and was trying to make me stand still and listen... It was as if God himself came to me and spoke:

'You are better than this. I never left you. Pick yourself up, son, find your mother. Your time has come. Everything precious is made with pressure: Gold, Diamonds, and minerals. Surrounded for many years undiscovered but now is your time to be uncovered and discovered. A pearl is precious but is made from the sand constantly irritating the clam at the bottom of the sea. Some come back from the bottom of the pits and rise. Find yourself, find Rodney and be free.'

From that moment on I started to fortify myself from the inside and prepared myself to emerge back to society. Before I get to the part of my story about my journey to find my mother and how it intensified. I want to bring you into the world of being homeless. What I used to call a bum, that is before I became a bum or what in dignity I wish to label as 'homeless'. My definition of being homeless is being lost within yourself a state of losing yourself while living in your own body. By choice of circumstances not at that time being able to live up to your full potential whether you have the mental ability to recognize this or if you are mentally depressed or oppressed. Not having the capacity of pulling yourself out of your dire situation. Of course not to be part of society at all.

Where I fit in was a little bit of all mentioned above. There was a period of my life that I just plainly did not like the hand that I was dealt and knew at that time had no power to overcome. The overwhelming odds against me which I chose to call civilization and judicial system which neither seemed civilized or fair. So I chose to live on my own merits and with my own set of rules. So from silver spoon to wooden spoon, I had become homeless. I met a lot of other individuals that were God given Angels. Pure in heart and too I met the demons of Satan on the cold dark streets of New York. But I shout out and remember each and everyone who lives in the streets who battle the elements in their mind. Little do people know how close they are to being homeless whether you live in a castle or a hole. To be homeless can be in a state of mind. You can be homeless from abandonment of love or loss of family or never having family, acts of nature or simply losing your job. No one is exempt. I know the pain, city to city, street to street, shelter to shelter, state to state. For some the cycle never stops. They die on the street in a cardboard box.

Chapter 16

Clear Mind

A S I STARTED to have more rational thoughts in my mind, my spirit kept telling me: *'Preston or Rodney when are you going to put this whole story together? You will never be whole until you follow your journey. Your know your name is Rodney Snell, but all the facts are hidden from you. You're identity is vanishing with time Rodney Snell you have to make a choice. Either you compromise and settle for what name you have been given and the identity given to you by the state of New York or What has been told to you that are you are Preston Jones and live with this lie for the rest of your life or you die trying to find out who you know you are, Rodney Snell?'* I decided to fight, fight, fight. I strapped up, put on my climbing gear, tied my boots and started my grueling journey out of hell. My goal was heaven, meaning the sky was the limit, to infinity and beyond. I then vowed to leave the dark cold pits of secrecy and come into the light. Expose and release all the pain and torment of the dark cold world that I had lived in order to move on I had to face the past and conquer it. Expose it all, all who had kept me in chains and bondage. It had to start with me and end with the State of New York. Ultimately, I knew I had to face the ultimate task master 'The New York State Judicial System."

———ᜃ♥ᜃ———

Chapter 17

The Search Begins

L ITTLE DID I know how intense this war against the state of New York's judicial system would be. All I knew is that I would be in a battle for my life and I couldn't give up on myself. Once again I started to make calls, and search for some kind of grounds and a trail of paperwork. I had to start somewhere, so I started back at Hospital were I was born in MT.Vernon New York. I called the records department to see if there was any information on a Rodney Snell born October 10th 1962. In their records of course she could not divulge any records to me because of HIPAA rules. I was infuriated because all I was trying to do is find out information about myself. I did understand her position because this was bigger than her. She could lose her job giving out that kind of information. So I asked if there was anything at all that she could tell me or any guidance. She told me, "Write vitals statistics in Albany, NY. Perhaps you can get additional help from them being that all adoptions in New York State would have been handled by them. That might be the best place for you to start."

I thanked her, and the receptionist stated: "You have an uphill battle Mr. Jones, good luck." I knew she was correct. How could I forget through my journey of addiction and self centered way of life. the one pain I could not forgive myself for was the passing of my son Preston Denard Jones. I was so caught up in my own world that I did not know that he needed a bone marrow transplant which I could have been a prime donor. My son passed at three and half years old and I had no knowledge of this until two hours after the funeral. I learned of this news from my mother's best friend. When I was high I would always try to keep out eye distance of all I knew who were not living the same destructive lifestyle as I was living. One day I was crossing through a short cut in an apartment building complex in White Plains and there dressed in black was my mother's best friend, her husband, and daughter. I was really high that day so of course I was just passing thru and wanted to be brief. I said hello and kept it moving then the daughter said, "Preston." I kept walking and she yelled out again, "Preston!" I kept my back toward them so as not to make eye contact I didn't want them to see my glassy eyes and see how high I was. These were respected religious friends that I knew my whole life and did not want this reported to my mother. *'I saw Preston and he was as high as a kite!'*

I stopped and said 'yes.'

"Where have you been?" She said. I barely glanced at them but made sure I made no eye contact. Then I heard, "Do you know where we are coming from?" It seemed like a slow motion eternal drag of emotional anticipation and time connected and intertwined with peril thoughts of confusion and wonder as the words came out of her mouth. It seemed as those words became pasted in still motion and invisible air. Dora said, "We are just coming back from your son's funeral." Oh my God. I froze in my tracks and I knew I had committed the ultimate felony, betrayal. Betrayal of not only my soul but of the soul of my son. I was dirt and there was no words or excuses that moment is branded in the memory of my every thoughts. As long as I breathe and have breath in my body the thought will be ever present to this day. I don't know where my son is buried. I must apologize but I am giving you the facts as they come to me because a lot of thoughts and feelings have simply been surpassed and pushed so far back that only now that I write them they resurface but as I stated earlier in this book is for you to feel what I feel, see what I see. This is me and who I am inside raped of love.

Back to the receptionist that stated this would be the journey of my life. I started back with Albany, NY, department of Vital Records. My thought was first try to get a birth certificate which would be my original one which stated my name was Rodney Snell and to find my mother's name on the certificate. Which would prove to be more difficult than I ever could have imagined. I was at the time living in Virginia beach with my adopted mother(Mildred) whom I came to take care of because of her failing health and knowing she was dependent on me and that I would never again let anyone close to me down as I had done my son. I kept my search for my biological mom a secret.

It was then January 2004, yes I could have just asked my mom who my biological mother was? What is her name? But that could have caused a major setback in her health and well being. She was dependent on and trusted me. So I deprived myself in order not to have her hurt. Seemed to me every time I thought about asking *'Mom, who is my mother?'* she had a seventh sense.

She would look at me and say, "Pressy, you're a good son. You're a good son, you'll miss me one day but I'm glad you came back home." So what was I supposed to do? I had to support her and sacrifice and suffocate my feelings for I still remember as a child she told me, *'I'd go to the ends of the Earth before I'd give you up.'* Somehow I knew that her journey on Earth was now very close to the end. So out of respect and care, I dared not cross that line and allow my mother the respect and peace to completely finish her journey before I fully entrenched myself in my grueling journey.

Chapter 18

The Legal Fight For My Rights

- *As stated before I started with Albany to try to get my original birth certificate. They only gave me the revised certificate stating my name was Preston Jones born to Theodore R. Jones and Mildred Jones. I knew this was not my original certificate.*

- *I called Mt. Vernon hospital where I was born. They told me they could not give me any information but I was told that my adoption was handle by the Department of Social Services in New York. it took me almost two years before I got any confirmation as to where in New York until I wrote over ten courts to find out that my adoption was thru Westchester County of Social Services.*

- *I wrote Westchester County Social Services. They explained that I had to contact the Surrogate Court of Westchester County.*

- *I wrote the Westchester County Surrogate Court. The court wrote back and explained to me that my records were sealed, meaning that I had no access to my own information.*

- *I wrote the court back and asked could they just give me the name of my mother or date of birth? They said they could not, that it was to protect my mother's identity. The only way to possibly find anything would be if I was one third American Indian or had a life threatening disease that would be my only option.*

- *I wrote the court back and filed a motion to unseal my adoption record based on my diagnosis of having multiple sclerosis. The court wrote me back and said I had to have medical proof from my doctor.*

- *I submitted a letter from my doctor proving that I was diagnosed with M.S. and I am currently under his care in the state of Virginia.*

- *The Surrogate Court of Westchester NY stated that since my case is sealed in the state of New York, I would have to have this diagnosis from a certified doctor who practices in the state of New York. So then I knew I had to make arrangements to travel from Virginia Beach to New York.*

- *While waiting to find a doctor in New York I knew I had to ask the court was there anyway to find out any information on how my adoption took place and if I had any family or siblings?*

- *The court wrote me back and said I had to file a motion for identifying information on my adoption, which I did.*

- *Six month later I received information on how my adoption took place and that my mother was too young to keep me because she had a child proceeding me a boy.*

- *So I wrote the court again and asked if there was anyway I could get more information on my mother and siblings.*

- *The Surrogate Court of Westchester responded that I'd have to submit another motion asking for identifying information on my mother and family.*

- *The court granted the Petition for Motion. I received identifying information but first I had to write the New York Department of Health and sign up for the adoption registry for information. This let the state legally allow any sibling that I had that might have signed onto the same registry to have access to my information. I would be in the database to be able to share information with them but of course they didn't know about me so that was a dead end.*

- *Got a registry number.*
- *Once I received my registry number then I received information such as:*

A. *My mother age: 17.*

B. *My mother's heritage: (African American) and that she was an United States Citizen.*

C. *Physical appearance: 5'3" approximately 100lbs*

D. *Hair color: Black and curly.*

E. *Skin color: Brown*

F. *Other characteristics: Attractive, well-groomed, very bright girl, demonstrates a warm personality.*

G. *Religion: Protestant.*

H. *Education, Occupation, talents.*

I. *Health and History of birth mother: She was in good condition at the time of adoptees birth and the was no record of any hereditary illness', mental or physical. She reported that she was from a family of six and born and raised in the south and that she had another child that was one years old at the time of my birth, which was also male.*

LET ME STOP for a moment so you can get your thoughts together just the same as I did. So now I am so grateful to know that my search was not in vain for now I had a physical description of what my mother looked like, her height, weight, skin complexion and she was petite with curly hair and that I had a brother. At the same time this added a million pounds of stress to every ounce of my mental and physical being because now in my mind I could see her even though they did not enclose any pictures of my mother. I could see her and feel her in my mind and still no information was given to me as to what her name was. This was mental torture to me.

Now I knew that I also have brother so if nothing else I surely will try to find him. He should still be alive being only one year older than me but then remember I still had no name. Also the paper stated that my mom was from a family of six. I didn't know whether her siblings were male or female but I knew this was a large family. So I have aunts and uncles out there. Now I was triple stressed but I geared up fortified my mind and concluded that a warrior had been born. Me against society, I appointed myself as general and the war began I vowed at that moment that this would be perhaps a suicide mission but that against all odds I would fight to find my mother, no bars or limits would keep me from my battle even if it meant dying for the cause. Failure was not an option. The first thing I had to do was change my mind set. No more emotions I had a job to accomplish I took love out of this equation and out of my heart. I took out sorrow, tears, disappointment, pain, fear. At the same time all joy and happiness and pleasure I ripped off. I reprogrammed my mind and body for one purpose, my mission to find my mother. To connect back to my life source my umbilical cord. My mission was now to feel my mother's heart beat next to mine. A hug, a touch, human contact which could only be restored by the one that started the process. (I knew in order to meet my goal, the journey must end with touching and seeing my mother.)

As if I were diseased ridden and needed to search the Earth for a cure. I searched for the cure to my diseases. The Messiah, Jesus, would be my mother all I needed to heal was one hug, one embrace, to be healed. All I needed was just to touch her. I wanted my imagination of what I pictured my mother to be since the age of five to come to life, to become reality. The frog needed the princess to give one kiss to come back to life I was the frog and my mom would be the princess. My dreams would be the reality. I needed to be greater than Martin Luther king who had dreams but never seeing the dreams come true. My dreams must become reality and then I promised that if I were granted this wish to find my mother that I would reach out to others by giving them hope not to give up. By telling my story and here it is. *(Back to the legal motions.)*

Remember when my adoption was sealed in the state of New York and I had to get a certified letter from a doctor in the same state saying that I had M.S.? So after my waiver of notice of petition for access to the sealed adoption record/consent (Domestic relations law- section 114, Adoption form 27A), I journeyed to New York from Virginia beach in 2011 to a specialist. I had a MRI of the brain and indeed once again their findings were that I had legions on the brain and gave me the diagnosis. I have remitting relapsing M.S. The doctor submitted a letter to the court stating that it would be beneficial to open my sealed adoption records. By opening my record it would enable me to have access to my family history to ensure proper treatment. So I had to send a motion in with that letter explaining to the Surrogate Court that: *because of medical reasons I would like to have my records unsealed. Also for personal reasons, I would like to know who my biological mother is.*

Two months later I received a letter back from the judge's chambers saying before they could even consider my motion that I would have to prove that my adoptive parents gave me permission to pursue this motion or that they were deceased and that I had to produce death certificates. I had my mother's death certificate but had no knowledge where my father had died because they had divorced in the eighties. I didn't have contact so I had to ask my mother's friends that were still alive if they had any knowledge of my dad's whereabouts. So after three months I got a call that my dad passed away in Robeson County, which was in Maxton, NC, in 1996. I called Robeson County and got my father, Theodore's death certificate. I submitted this information to the court. Three months after that I received a letter from the court stating that the word 'beneficial' was not good enough to unseal my records.

The doctor stated it would be 'beneficial' to open my records. The court said that I could repeal this decision but I would have to show that my disease was life threatening in order to unseal my records. At this time I was totally stressed and discouraged and really angry with the whole judicial system. All I wanted was to know who I was and where I came from and to find my family.

Later in 2011, I appealed that motion and went back to New York. I had to go through the same procedures, MRI and full exam from a different doctor. This time this doctor was in Pelham, NY, Westchester County. The doctor examined me and came to the conclusion that: *'it would be extremely necessary to know Mr. Jones genetic breakdown to properly treat him.'* Once again I submitted this letter and was denied. The court said that saying 'extremely necessary' was not good enough to unseal the record. Meanwhile I went to my best friend Timothy Williams and asked for help. He helped me launch a Facebook page to reach the mass network of people. There I submitted live videos trying to find my mother. On YouTube I put a series of videos begging for help and anyone knowing the Snell name. You can find these videos under 'Where are you, Mommy?' and 'Man Searches for His Mom More Than 50 years.'

I wrote a play one day of exactly how I believed my adoption took place. I practiced it with characters, which I was going to produce and shoot a video and put it on YouTube. I started a GoFundMe page, which no donations came to. I was trying to cover my expenses going back and forth to New York, but I guess my story seemed unreal. One more time about six months later I went back to New York to the doctor in New Rochelle, NY. This was a office very small. It smelled like vomit in the hallways, they still filled their files in the vanilla envelopes, no computers. I started to walk out of the office because I was appalled by the conditions of it. Just when I was about to walk out the doctor called me. He sat me down and asked, "Mr. Jones, how can I help you? Seems like you've come an awful long way just to see me. All the way from Virginia Beach to New York?"

"Yes I came from Virginia, my records are sealed in the state of New York. I have M.S. and I have been turned down three times on my petition to unseal my adoption record." I said. The doctor looked at me for what seemed an eternity. Even though I vowed not to have any emotions, my eyes were full of water. I knew that he is pretty much my last chance for now because I had exhausted my money over the years coming back and forth to New York paying each time I had to get a MRI. This ran into thousands and hotel fare and rental car fees, I was broke now.

The doctor examined me again, then he examined my records and papers that I had from the other doctors. He said to me, "Mr. Jones, from the paper trails, I have no doubt and I am fully convinced that you have M.S. What seems to be the problem?" I showed him the responses and denials from three previous attempts. He sat there for a moment and looked at the name of the judge that was presiding over my cases and that kept denying my petition. He said, "I know this judge, I treated his mother for M.S. I can't believe this, let me talk to my lawyer and see how I must word this correctly." I thanked him and went back to Virginia Beach.

In October of 2012 on the 31st, the doctor called me to tell me he had sent me a letter and that I would receive it in the mail within a few days. Now this seemed like an eternity waiting for this letter finally I received the letter stating that:

It is 'imperative medically' that the sealed adoption records must be unsealed pertaining to the medical aspects of Mr. Jones's biological parents and siblings.

I submitted this to the court. In February, I received a letter that this matter would be placed on the calendar for March 27th 2013. Now I knew I had thirty two days to wait for the answer to what could be the decision of my life time, that I prayed, fought, cried, and dreamed for. It was finally here: Preston Jones against the State of New York Surrogate's Court of Westchester.

On February 27th 2013 I received a letter from the court stating that my motion to unseal my adoption records was granted for medical purposes and that I would be appointed a Guardian ad Litem, which mean I cannot personally look in my adoption file, the court appoints a lawyer to look into my file and retrieve information pertaining to my case. They will contact or at least attempt to contact my biological mother if she is still living. I was overcome with a stream of emotions a feeling of victory, but still very optimistic as to what would be the outcome of this search. I was still not trusting that the Guardian ad Litem was going to do her job up to par and be as diligent as I had been to get this far up the mountain. For if this person did not do their job I'd be back at the bottom and would have to make my descend back up again.

On March 1st 2013, I received a letter from the Guardian ad Litem introducing herself as the lawyer that would be personally looking into my adoption records. Her office was in Hasting on the Hudson in New York. Even though I should have been ecstatic with joy, a black, gloom remained over my spirit and I didn't know why.. I guess you call that the sixth sense.

After twenty nine days I received a call from the guardian, she explained to me that the court approved a payment of three thousands dollars for her legal services. I paid it April 3rd 2013. I received a call from her she stated, "Mr. Jones, I have done a diligent search of eight point five hours and although I did find your mother's name and information I could not locate her. Your mother and father were both Mexican immigrants. I am so sorry."

My heart and my hopes sank with that thought, I was hurt. For a fleeting moment I had lost hope. My mind, body, and soul, felt a void, empty and homeless destitute. Without hope I felt as if the whole world in which I tried to build all my hopes, dreams, and desires, had been set ablaze. I felt the same as a person coming home to their house that is ablaze in fire. All that I had worked so hard for over 50 years was burning before my eyes. All hopes of finding my family was gone. Time froze in stagnant misery. I could not bare the stab and rip in my heart. This pain was unbearable and deep but yet I could not produce a tear. The guardian said "I'm so sorry Mr. Jones, but Mexico is out of our jurisdiction."

I asked, "Ma'am can you at least give me a name? What is my mother's name, can you at least tell me that?"

She replied, "No. In five days you will get notification that this matter is concluded. Once I submit my findings to the judge."

Chapter 19

Leave No Stone Unturned

ONCE I GOT my thoughts together, I started thinking 'This can't be the way it's going to end?' I went back thru all of my paperwork from day one. I sat down and reviewed each and every motion, every docket, all the paper from Vitals Statistics and right in front of me was my answer. In 2008 I had received un-identifying information and identifying information that plainly stated that my mother was an United States citizen. So how could my mother and father be Mexican immigrants? Impossible. This lawyer was trying to throw me off of my trail. She had deceived me, she lied to me and tried to turn my whole world upside down.

I had the proof that I needed but now my case was the final order. After many nights tossing and turning I could no longer settle for this defeat. I had to fight, fight to the end. I had to gear up once again. Strip my mind of all fears, all tears, all negative vibes, and all emotions. I once again ripped all happiness, all joy, all emotional aspects of human feelings. I surrounded myself in Plexiglas, I could see all but allowed no feelings or emotions in. Nothing could penetrate me, I had become the sniper in the jungle. I had to one by one pick off my enemies to survive. I know that I was dying inside from all the stress. I was no more than a walking zombie, shoot me and I felt no pain. I had to keep going. My head was so tight with anxiety, it felt like a thousand rubber bands intertwined and wrapped around my head as tight as humanly possible.

At that point in my life, I not only became suicidal but homicidal. My mind was blown all my thoughts were borderline insanity. I fully understood what a martyr meant I was ready to die for my cause. Like that. I then fully understood the thinking of a terrorist for a terrorist is against society usually because the Government has wronged them or because of a personal injustice to them or their family or their religious sect. I knew that I would never be able to find my mother with these thoughts. I wanted to go to that lawyer's office and put a gun to her head and tell her to tell me the truth about what was actually in my adoption file or should I just blow her house up? I fully understood that the thought of a terrorist, no matter who they harm or kill, they believe in their cause and die with pride. I was right there but with the few fibers of sanity I had suppressed this and knew that this would defeat my purpose. I would never feel my mother's heart beat or feel her hug or love. It seemed that I had become so insane that I had lost my membrane. Picture that I was the explosive truck containing the bomb hoping that I had enough fortification to hold the force of detonation. So as I pushed this anger and resentment of the judicial system into my toes, I knew what I had to do. I had to expose this the legal way.

Chapter 20

The Fight To Expose

AUGUST 23ᴿᴰ, 2013 I wrote the judge that was presiding over this case that had close my decision of order. It read as follows:

Most Honorable Judge, I enclose this letter to you because I believe and know if you have the knowledge of King Solomon, you have the wisdom to know when something is not correct. That is your job as a judge to make correct decisions based on the facts and all though I am handwriting this letter to you, and all my punctuations and spelling might not be correct, I somehow believe you have the perception, wisdom, and knowledge to read between the lines.

Therefore I submit to you a copy of my adoption and medical, non identifying report, which clearly states that my mother is a United States citizen. This information I have proves without a shadow of doubt, that my mother was not a Mexican immigrant. So I am prepared to submit this information to all public entities including the newspaper. Here I have submitted a copy of this registry to you I therefore feel and know that the Guardian ad Litem that you appointed for resolving my case did not represent my best interest or have my best well being intended for me and has misrepresented your court. I there by ask and beg the court to investigate this matter and after finding that I am correct. That the court repetition to reopen my case and files in order that due process be properly administered to my case.

Almost two years later, after continuous letters to the court July 29th, 2015 I received a new letter from a different Guardian and the court granting reopening of my case. A new judge was appointed to preside over my case. In August I received confirmation from the courts that they have contacted my biological mom, Corzie Dean Hughes. I guess you can imagine how happy I was that I had continued to fight for what I believe in. I know that this story is jumping around but actually I had taken my wife Lisa away on a weekend getaway in Williamsburg, Virginia and I was on Facebook and my first message arrived.

'I am Yolanda, your first cousin... I am Jamie your niece.... I am Nicole your sister.... I am Bridgette your sister... I am Katherine your sister... I am Robin your sister...'

At first I didn't believe this, I typed 'Stop playing with my emotions and stop playing games.' My wife Lisa told me I better see who it was. It was real! It took me two hours before I could respond. Once I contacted them we talked from six that evening to about two or three in the morning. The letter from the courts, stating that they had officially found my mother came about two weeks later. Like I said before the court already contacted my mother but legally the information had to be official through stamp and sealed typed decision. Thanks to my friend Timothy Ivan Williams, I had a Facebook set up 'Preston Jones' and they searched and found me. How grateful I am to all that helped me in my struggle. The purpose of this book is to help others who are trying and struggling to find their love ones. Don't let anyone tell you that it is impossible to find your biological mother or father or siblings. You must fight for you because at the end of the day they know their family, they know their mother and father, but you don't know yours.

I was forced to waited fifty four years to know my mother. Fifty four years to hug my mom and in the same breath a lot of people have the fear of disappointment that might come with the territory but please continue your searches. Expand your horizons. If you don't fight for yourself who will? Who can fight for you like you can fight for yourself? Remember ninety five percent of people going through this process don't know even where to start. You start with your heart. Take your time, remember that most people looking on will not understand what you are going through. Your first mindset is to understand that they can only empathize or sympathize. Unless they are wearing your shoes and walking the same path, then they can not feel exactly what you feel. So understand and ignore them. And until you can understand that they can't understand your pain and what you're going through and feeling what you're feeling then you will never be able to forgive them. Don't help everyone fulfill their dreams and you don't fulfill your own. I did this search with blood sweat and tears. You have computers and technology so use it to your advantage.

The answer to your question is there! The pieces to your puzzle is there for you to find and when you find it you will know how it fits and when to fit it in. Don't wait on time for time does not wait on you. I also took a DNA test with Ancestry and 23 and me. This helped cover all the bases.

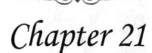

Chapter 21

The Relationship

O N THURSDAY AUGUST 20th, 2015, my wife Lisa and I drove to Greensboro, NC to physically meet my(Corzie Snell Hughes) mother. Life as I had known it for fifty two years would forever, once again, be altered. This would be the ultimate feeling of self gratification and the ultimate high and most satisfying quench for the lifetime of fifty two years of thirst. At 3:32 in the afternoon on Thursday August 20th, 2015, I walked in my mother's house. I was finally at home, I was at peace. I embraced my mom and in the instant of my first embrace with my mother I felt my heartbeat as one with my mother's. It seemed as though I was born again.

Brought back fifty four years back to the future. I tried to absorb all of my mother's love like a parched desert plant that finally received the first spring rain. I sucked every drop of love that I could from her. In that one time suspended hug I felt myself connect by the umbilical cord and promised to never let her go and thanks be only to my God, Jehovah, that he rose me above all to have this humbling yet life changing experience.

There also I laid my eyes on my sisters, Nicole, Robin, Kathy, and Bridgette. I finally had a family not only that but I have another sister Yvonne, and a brother, Kenny. Plus I met my nieces and nephews, Erika, Jamie, Ashley, Destiny, Steve, Dorian, Arthur, Tion and Jeremiah from nothing and no family to so many that I couldn't remember all the names. What a blessing. Now my relationship with my mother is great we talk everyday two or three times a day. I make sure I call in in the morning to say good morning and each and every night to say good night. My mother and I have had many discussions on what it would have been like to grow up together in the same house.

My sister Robin (whom I have given the name little mama) took me on a tour of the town in Bassett Virginia, where I would have grown up and been raised at I actually got to set foot on the property where the actual house is still standing. I try to keep in contact with my sisters each week some I call every day. It is the strangest thing though, it seems as if I have always been in the family. I am treated like any sisters would treat their brother. We argue and we fight just like any siblings would but at the end of the day I am happy to say they are my sisters. I love them all and would not give them up for the world. In my search I have met many cousins. Lynn from Connecticut, I love with my heart, she is absolutely wonderfully loving. So is my cousin that lives in Atlanta, Yolanda. Gai Gai and Doris just to name a few.

I am very grateful though to my adopted mother for teaching the principals to stay afloat and the spirit of never giving up and determination. I thank you mom so much for that and may your legacy always continue to be immortalized. I thank God for giving me two moms, one to raise and guide me and one to see what I have become and to know under the circumstances that she made the right choice.

I am in no way angry or insulted that my mother had to give me up for adoption. I am very grateful that she has accepted me back into the family. I feel that by the hard work to get back and find my mother, that yes, it has given me a VIP pass to heart. but since the age of five from the moment that she was first mentioned to me she had exclusive rights to my heart.

I felt as though this whole process has and will continue to be a healing process to my mother as well as myself. It's complicated but at the same time very simple in my mind. My mother had to have a void in her heart for fifty four years from the moment that I was taken from her and given to another. The healing for me is just so obvious. I had been look for her for over fifty years and my heart literally leaked blood for her and now my pain has been healed and I have her to love now. Now my sleepless nights are replaced with peaceful thoughts and dreams of satisfaction.

Chapter 22

The Scars

WAR CAUSES MANY scars as we all know. Here lies some of my many scars in which I realized and once again these are just the facts of my scars. The one thing I know is that I have lost and diligently working on trust issues and that includes trusting myself. As stated before I knew that I am still holding onto a thin layer of Plexiglas as protection. I know that I had a mother growing up but not a mommy.

My mother (Mildred) was an excellent mother. She provided and cared for me physically and I had no physical wants but emotions was not there. Now I still crave the mommy part the emotional part of love but it is hard to give it or accept it. My wife craves the emotional love but I find myself incapable of fully fulfilling that task. I love my wife and will provide all that I can materially but I know that I am starving her emotionally and it almost seems that I am incapable of emotions. I have put my wife through so much while I was on this journey. While I was trying to find myself and I was so engrossed in my search for love and my family that in this process I raped my wife of love. I snatched the little emotions and physical affection from her while on my journey and to accomplish my goal of finding my mother. I jeopardized and starved my wife of the very fabric in which I was searching for which was love. So I publicly apologize to my wife for the self inflicted rape of love. I thank Jehovah that Lisa has stood by me through this grueling journey and I am sorry that while I was looking for the healing that I ripped your soul and will do what I must to heal the tear and deep scar that

I have caused. I thank you for being such a strong and understanding wife and sorry for the pain that I caused you Lisa. I am forever grateful for your patience and hopefully you're reading this book for the first time. Also Thank you Lisa for keeping up to your vows of faithfulness through better or worse. I love you.

Another scar which came as a result of this situation was that I had suppressed and stuffed and forgot major things of importance. Going back to the beginning of my story remember that I had found two envelopes in that brown box in the basement? My mom told me to put the other envelope back in the box? Well that other envelope was the paperwork for my brother. That envelope contained his adoption records. I had kept that a secret for over fifty years. I never uttered a word to him. In other words my brother was not my brother. I had totally blocked this out of my mind until after my grueling journey to find my mom was complete. I still possessed that original document stating my brother's birth name and adoption file on the date of January 15th 2016. I searched for my brother and once I found his address and number I had to make the decision whether I let him live his life not knowing that we weren't biological brothers or do I just continue to hold the secret? After careful thought and many sleepless nights I came to the conclusion that I had to heal and most of all end the cycle of secrets.

Now I had not heard his voice or seen him since my age of thirteen. I had to track him down through his state I.D. number because he had done many years in the Prison System. From that number I was able to find his parole officer. I asked his parole officer if he had a client by the name of Wilton Jones he told me he couldn't disclose that information. I told him that Wilton was my brother and that I had not seen him since I was thirteen and if there was anyway that he could give him my number I would appreciate it. Five minutes later the phone rang it was Wilton. "Preston? Where the hell have you been?"

We talked then I asked him for his address. He told me that he still lived in a parole house I told Wilton, that I had some mail that our mother wanted him to have. I sent him pictures of us growing up as young children and sent him pictures of me from a child to adulthood. I also sent him pictures of our mom and dad (Mildred and Theodore) and his original birth certificate stating his birth name. I knew it was the only right thing to do was to let Wilton know the truth. He would have the right to search for his parents but yet he had his right to know that he was not my biological brother.

I made no contact with him for three months. When I called him he seemed unaffected by the adoption records all he said was "You are my real brother as far as I am concerned." We now talk on the phone quite often. The reason I tell you these facts is so that you understand that there are a lot of other factors that weigh in when you choose to find your biological parents. Not all parents are just going to accept you in their families because you have decided that you want to know who your mother or father or siblings are. Although in my case with my mother and siblings I was rewarded with their love and blessings. It is not always the case. A lot of times they have gotten on with their lives and have other families or don't expect that you would pop into their lives. Some parents give up their children because they simply didn't want them and some just could not afford them/ They may have been a victim of rape. All that I am saying is that be determined in your search but be aware of the downfalls and that even though you might want acceptance you might not be accepted.

Some families have moved on with their lives and Pandora's box is sometimes best left closed as you might find out in the next chapter.

Chapter 23

Pandora's Box

This is the actual box of my adoption papers.

I TRULY KNOW that finding my mother was a unique blessing, although there was a lot of perseverance and pain involved. At what point do you just praise God and thank him and be satisfied for the gift given to you? This is where I had issues.

I was and am very grateful for Jehovah for granting of my ultimate wish, my ultimate dream and fulfillment of a life long battle after mental anguish to have my mother's heart beat next to mine. To feel her love. This should have been what they say a happy ending to a long story. God blessed you and your new found life with your new found family. Learn to love your mom and continue to enjoy the blessings of being accepted. Remember this was my only ambition to find my mother. Yes I recognized the greatness of all that I had accomplished and the great struggle to get where I am at now. As far as now, having even a mental sanity in my mind the extreme release of the intense tension being relieved. My thoughts of insanity had become sane and rational. Now what a blessing and feeling of calmness and comfort a feeling of being complete and almost becoming a whole person again. To know where I came from and to know and see where I was protected for nine months, preparation for my entry into the world at last. I knew and had a closure to the many sleepless nights as a five year old child to the age of fifty four of wondering what it would be like to have that hug that I had been waiting for so many years from my mother. There was now a healing that I finally knew my mother's name, Corzie Snell. Now I could permanently brand her picture in my mind and would never forget my mother's facial features. Now I could finally match the many images that flashed through my mind of my mother's statue.

The many images of how I thought my mother's voice would sound like. The many images that a young child of five with a vivid imaginary mind would have the many images of my mom being my imaginary friend became a reality. Those late nights lying lonely in the dark imagining happy thoughts of how my family life would have been if I only knew who my mother was. Those hugs that I held back from my adopted mother because I so desperately wanted to save a portion of that love for my mom Corzie Snell. Now I could hug her, she could feel my love and no one would take that away from me. I fought too hard to find it. My healing process now began with me finding my mother and added family of a brother and five loving sisters. I could start to feel the healing process begin from the inside starting in my heart. I felt as if the first man Adam did when he was presented with his wife, Eve. This was at last flesh of my flesh, bones of my bones. My mom is everything and more than I could have imagined. At the same time my imagination was not far off from the actual person that physically that I thought her physical characteristics were. So I say all of that to say I appreciated all those facts but I still quenched, like I said I was almost whole. I was and am happy but had one more issue for a complete healing and a fill of the void of my quest still left. That was "Who is my father?"

Now this is where Pandora would or could take full effect. Now fifty four years again in my basement I opened that brown 'Pandora's box' and went on the journey of a lifetime and was fortunate to come out alive and on top of the hill because I found my mother. I survived the traps and mazes and tricks, puzzles and riddles of finding my mother. I was victorious and successful because not only did I find my mother but my mother and my family accepted me with open arms and love. In my mind I knew that perhaps I should be happy with the unpresidential result of what that Pandora's box had offered me. I knew that all rationality says if you survived Pandora's box once then just close the box, seal it, and throw all the pain and years of mixed emotions back and keep the happiness. I thought, *'Preston lock the box and throw away the key and all traces of the contents. Let it sink to the bottom of the sea. Never to be opened again. Preston you have been through enough, leave the father issues alone and be satisfied don't ruin your blessing.'* What would I do? I didn't want to jeopardize the wonderful hours of conversation and bonding that my mother and I were having. I didn't want to jeopardize the relationship that I was enjoying with my sisters. I didn't want to jeopardize my relationship with my baby sister Bridgette, we talk everyday, two or three times. Yet I needed to at least know my father's name but at the same time I did not want them to think that I wasn't satisfied with them. I had only known them at that point a few months but in my mind I knew I would not truly be happy until I at least attempted to give this my complete attention.

I thought, *'Preston, you can't solve and close a case without all the facts!'* I wasn't satisfied with this becoming a cold case. I decided to find out all the facts. My final decision was to keep the case open. A good detective looks at all the leads and facts.

Chapter 24

Pandora's Box Reopened

I CALLED MY mother and asked "Mama? Do you have any information on my father? I am not trying to press my luck but I would like to know." My mom paused for a moment then said.

"Yes, boy, I know who your father is, but I don't want you to get hurt trying to find him and you know you might be opening a can of worms" and she paused.

I said, "Mama I know." Mama told me my father's name and then I said, "Tell me how you met him. Now Pandora's box was reopened.

"Well I met your dad in Mt. Vernon, New York. We rented an apartment upstairs from your dads uncle."

"Well thank you mom." I said and then asked. "What happened to him during your pregnancy?" My mom said once she told my father that she was pregnant, then my dad disappeared and my mom was unable to take care of me on her own because she already had a child. My mother said she wanted to keep me but would not have a choice because she still lived with her mother and she would not allow her to keep me. My mom desperately wanted to keep me but could not afford to so her mother made her give me up for adoption.

"I know you are going after your father now. I know you are a very persistent person." My mom said and paused. There was a silence and a off settle sarcastic sound in her voice. "Could you do me a favor?"

"What would that be?" I asked.

"When you find your father can you slap him for me?" I asked her why she said, "For him just leaving me and forcing me to put you up for adoption. He gave me no support and skipped out on his responsibility." So here is you public smack from mom to you father, if you are reading this right now. My mother also said that when she gave birth to me at the hospital, how very sad she was thatI had to be given up for adoption she had no choice, her mother made that decision because my mother was under age. My mother wished that by being adopted I would be given the things and love that I needed in order to turn out to be the best individual that I could possibly be. My mom then told me that she noticed that after she had me that she noticed the head nurse on that shift had left and went home for the night. My mom asked the new nurse on shift could she hold me one last time because she knew it would be the last time that she would see me. My mother was not supposed to see me after she gave birth to me. The procedure then was to take the baby at birth and not let the mother get any kind of emotional attachments to the child. Remember this was 1962.

So the nurse brought me to my mom and my mother said that she held me up and looked at me, hugged me, kissed me, and told me, "Never and I mean never forget your name, Rodney. Rodney Snell, I know one day you will find me." Sometimes I wonder if that was what impelled me to find her? As if a child, a root or hex, was placed on me that kept turmoil in my soul until I met her expectations. That I was able to find her. Was that was my determination was about? Was that what the drive and possessive nature of this search was or the combination of a self induced spell of love? Some secrets you never get a true answer to. Some are just as they are, untouchable. Now my feelings were mixed. I had my mother's approval to find my dad and knew that it would or at least should not interfere with life as it had been to this moment as regards to our relationship. Which meant a lot to me being that my mom is the matriarch of the family. I have her blessings and so I can go to war if I need be. With her blessings which meant so much to me with her understanding then the rest will understand. With her acceptance, then the rest of the tribe, the family, accepts. So win, lose, or draw I was back on the quest for knowledge for the completion of my ancestry hoping that I might complete my circle of love. In the back of my mind, I had my doubts for I knew that there is a thing called maternal love, a mother's love, which is one of the strongest driving forces of human nature. The love of a mother. When it comes to paternal or fatherly love the percentage diminishes. I guess most men it is just a moment of pleasure and then they go about with life, unbothered just passing on the lineage. Keeping their names going, keeping a legacy, But a mother receives and holds inside and the life has to be nurtured and the baby depends on the mother for life. The mother gives the baby protection and prepares him for entry to the outside world. So I guess that's what makes the difference between most fathers is the man ejaculates and let it out but the mother receives and lets the love in and feels the effect of intimacy inside of her and the result is love and growth. All combined and enter the baby straight through the protected life tube the umbilical cord. Twenty four hours a day a mother feels the growth and love. She is the designed protector of that soul. So in essence, if I could locate my father, then it would be my mission to find out if he was just a sperm donor or if he would step up to the plate to be my dad.

Chapter 26

The Search for My Father

WELL HERE WE go knowing my father's name and the last known addre in Mt. Vernon from fifty four years ago. That's where I needed to start. I became pretty good at this now so I called the Department of taxes in Mt. Vernon, New York because this is public information. I talked to the clerk, she gave her the address and asked who paid the taxes in 1962 at that address. The clerk was able to give me names for the next forty plus years. The house changed hands from my father or at least the name my mother gave me. So I knew that part was correct. His name was on the tax document.

From there I did a people's search with that name and address and the site said that my father had lived in Mt. Vernon, New York and moved to Wyndover Woods, Greenburgh, NY, remember I grew up in Greenburgh. There was a address presently in North Carolina Now the web site gave me phone numbers and addresses for all three locations. I called the Mt. Vernon numbers and of course these three number did not exist. It had been over fifty years. I called the number in Greenburgh, which is located outside of White Plains, about an half hour from where I was born in Mt. Vernon. That number was out of service. I looked up another site and it gave me the name of people that might be related to my father and children, one boy and two girls. According to their birthdates, I would if this was my father, would be the first born.

Now all the facts geographically fit. All his previous locations were all in a fifty mile radius from where I was conceived and born. The last location showed up as possibly living in North Carolina, which kind of puzzled me but being that all of the other information seemed to match. I called my mother and asked her did she know where my dad's family originated from? She said she wasn't sure but she believed North Carolina. So after weeks of searching, I was able to pinpoint an exact address in North Carolina because they gave me three possible locations and to me everything seemed to come in sync. The tax record of the house to him moving to Greenburgh. Because my adoption records stated that my father worked in an operating room in the hospital and I knew there were three hospitals in that area, White Plains Hospital, St. Agnes, and Mt. Vernon, where I was born.

I halted that part of the research and started calling the three hospitals, one hospital told me that he had worked at that hospital but because of HIPPA laws, they couldn't give me any information. Then I believed that I was on the right trail but where did North Carolina fit in and could I actually have other siblings? Oh my heart was beating and palms were sweating. I picked up the phone and started with the 910 area code. The phone rang and rang but no answer. I called back for the next four days. I tried again April 12th 2016, someone answered it was a woman, she sounded to be an older woman. So I said, "Hello ma'am. Please don't hang up. I know this might sound crazy but does a Johnny Moore live there?"

"What is this in reference to?" She asked.

"Well ma'am my name is Preston Jones born Rodney Snell, I was adopted October 10th 1962 at Mt. Vernon Hospital and I am looking for my biological father." I replied. She said.

"Well what makes you think that this is the right house that you are calling?" So I told her because my mother, Corzie Snell, told me that without a doubt that my father's name was Johnny Moore. The lady asked me again what my name was, where I was born and what date was I born on, and my mother's name. I repeated back everything that I told her before. Then she paused for about a minute as if she were trying to put it all together and calculate the timing of conception. She then said, "Preston, I am sorry, but you don't belong here. You are not a part of this family. I am sorry that I can't help you, I am sorry."

"Thank you ma'am. I have a feeling that I do and I am going to highlight and circle you name and I am sure that I will be back in contact with you." She hung up the phone. I sat there for about ten minutes and said to myself, *'Preston, I have a feeling that you belong in that family.'* It was all down in my gut and my soul. I continued to other areas of research with that name Moore and research took me to Ohio and many other states. Even in Europe but all the while I kept looking back on that information that I had highlighted and each time my stomach would turn as if my body was telling me, *'Preston you know this is where you came from and where your kin are too.'* I just couldn't shake it.

Months passed and I got back on my Ancestry DNA and 23 and Me and posting that if anyone knew any Moore Family to please contact me. I also went to find a grave and family reunions for the Moore Family online. I tried to friend all the Moore to see what information was there but still dead ends. I constantly mentioned these facts to my youngest sister Bridgette who lives in Detroit. One day as usual she called me and we were on the phone talking for about two hours. She is very long winded but I love her. Bridgette says to me. "Peewee (her nickname for me) What's your daddy's name again?

"Johnny Moore," I said, "Bridgette are you driving. I told her to look for it when she got home. Ten minutes later she called me back yelling.

"Peewee!" Oh my God, I thought she had gotten into an accident.

"What's wrong Bridgette?"

"I found your Daddy. I found your Daddy!"

"How do you know?" I asked. Bridgette said she got online and found some numbers on People Search and Bridgette called and spoke to a woman, and at first Bridgette said that the lady said no, I'm sorry your brother does not belong in our family. The lady had the phone on speaker. My sister Bridgette said a voice from the background said your brother "Preston is my first born and I know Corzie and her brothers and sister, Sank and Hortense. We lived in the same building in Mt. Vernon."

My sister Bridgette she asked him was he okay with her telling me that she found him because I was hurt enough, just with that ordeal of finding our mother. She told him that me and her were very tight. She didn't want to see me hurting anymore. "If I could tell him to call you, are you going to be a part of his life?"

"Yes you can tell him to call me. I will be a part of his life." He said. I thanked my sister and asked her for the number. When she gave me the number, the strangest feeling came over me. I said that number sounds familiar. I opened my book that I had done my research in and found the number that I already had in my book circled and the same address. This was the same house and phone number that I had called and was denied. Every ounce of information that I had given her this was the same person that my sister called. My gut was right! I began to wonder why the denial?

I called the number and I got an answer. "Hello?" the voice asked. I paused for a moment, going back to my memory, I thought to myself, *'This is the same woman I spoke to when I first called and the lady told me that I don't belong in that family. This was the same woman that was asking me repetitively what my name was, when was I born, and who my mother was? What hospital? This was the same person, when I told her that I would circle the name and number in my book and that I was sure that I would be back in contact with.'* I stated to her, "My name is Rodney Snell. My sister called and my dad, Johnny Moore confirmed that he was my dad."

A silence came over the phone, then she started yelling at the top of her voice, "You should have left this alone! I don't like you, you're arrogant and you don't listen! Why can't you just leave us alone?" I understood what she was saying but I just could not leave it at that so I said.

"Ma'am, I am not trying to be rude or disrespectful in any matter or fashion. You don't have to like me but if you gave me a chance, then maybe you would get a chance to know me."

"I don't want to know you!" She yelled. Then a voice came in.

"Preston, this is Johnny Moore. I am your father but you have disturbed my whole family. Don't call back here until the times is right!."

I paused for a moment and asked, "Well, when will the time be right? I've been waiting 54 years for the right time, which is now."

"I'll let you know when the time is right." I asked him when that will be, "When I call you. Now I have a lot of problems in my house because of you."

I immediately asked, "Well sir, whom shall I call you or address you as?"

"Anyway you want just don't call me. I'll call you."

"Well Dad, do I have any siblings?"

"Yes, you have 3, two sisters and a brother."

"Do they know about me?"

"No, I haven't told them that will take time. I am going to hang up. Remember, don't call here until I call you." He hung up. I had already done my homework and knew of my siblings, which was found on Facebook. I made contact with one of my siblings, my brother of whom was a lawyer in Detroit. I called his law office and asked to talk to Mr. Moore, but that was his answering service. They asked who I was? I just told them that I was just a client that needed to discuss some confidential information. The answering service said they would forward my number to him. About an hour later my phone rang and my brother answered the phone and said, "This is Moore Law Offices, can I help you?"

"Hello sir, first I wanted to make sure that this is a good time to talk being the personal matter of this conversation."

"Sure it is." So I introduced myself my name as Preston Jones.

"You and I share the same father. I am actually older than you. You would be my baby brother." Once again there was dead air.

"Hold on I need a moment to get myself together." At the same time my call waiting was beeping, it was my father on the other line. I clicked over he said not to bother or call my brother. I told him it was too late I already told him and I was currently on the other line. Informed him that I needed to clear the line. Once I was back over to the other line my brother continued.

"I knew nothing of this. Does my mother know about this?"

"Yes she does. She just finished cussing me out."

"Let me call you back, I need to talk to my mother and see if she's okay because I know this has to be a shock to her."

"Okay, we'll talk."

"I am Buddhist and will embrace the truth, then I will embrace it, but I won't cross my mother. I'll be in touch." As time went on perhaps two months passed, I tried to call my father to just say hello and try to create a relationship with him. It seemed as though they were screening the calls. I reached out and tried to friend my two sisters on Facebook and received no response. This baffled me. How long was I supposed to wait? I had the final piece to my puzzle in my hand to complete my life's journey but my father and siblings were not giving me any acknowledgment it's like being that I had been a secret once again for fifty four years. They were trying to keep me a secret and sweep me under the rug like I never existed. I definitely did not want to be swept under the rug. I was at the point in my life that I want to be liberated, no sooner than two months later, I got a message from my father.

I guess to reassure his motion to "make sure that you don't call this house until I call you because what you did was borderline harassment." That just blew me away when I heard that I am trying to put the fact of my life together and the man who is supposed to be my father is now telling me that I am harassing him. Pandora all the way. So I started texting my brother simply good night, each night and after a while he'd just text me good night. So I was starting to make progress with him slowly. We had small conversations, then they stopped. I left messages and got no responses back. So I thought to myself I guess this is really wasted energy. I must concentrate on the relationship with my father about two months later, I wrote my father a letter from my heart and mailed it to that he would receive it on Father's day. Here I was hoping for a response good or bad and indeed, he did call me when he called me he said, "Preston, this is Mr. Moore."

"What's up, Dad?"

"Listen I told you don't call here. Now you're writing me, now you are harassing me. Listen I am not your father!" It took me back for a minute. I had to regroup, so I asked my father,

"So now you're telling me that you are not my father? Which is it? Your are my father or you're not?"

"You are not my son and I am not your father is what I am telling you. Is that clear enough for you to understand? I'll say it one more time so you can understand, Preston. You are *not* my son!" I was so hurt and devastated but somehow I felt that my father was just trying to throw me off my square.

So I asked my father, "Would you be willing to give me DNA because in one breath you say you're my father, then in the next, you say that you are not. So if you are my father then the truth will come out and if you are not my father then you truly don't ever have to worry about me in life again. Is that a deal?"

"I don't want to take a DNA test, I am telling you that you ARE NOT my son! That's final!" That was a devastating blow to me but I'm not one to give up and at that moment I knew that Pandora's box was fully open. My father called back ten minutes later and said. "Take all that stuff that you have on your Facebook off your site. We are a very private and Christian family. So before I was able to establish myself in my father's family, I had already been ostracized and rejected so back to Ancestry DNA. I went searching and found that there were actually test that I could take to separate my paternal DNA from my maternal DNA and being that I have found my mother and my mother submitted her DNA. Then I had to have my dad's DNA separate, which would be done by taking a Y chromosome DNA test, this would show only my father's DNA. If anyone is related to my father on his side it will show up. That's if anyone on my father's side has taken the same test. Also I have inquired of a few lawyers to see what the laws of statute of limitation is in Columbia, SC to see if I can actually subpoena my father to take the test. This is on the strength of having a life threatening disease and apparently there is no statute of limitations. As regards to age that I have to force my father to submit to a DNA test courts ordered in New York, it would be eighteen. I have retained a lawyer in Columbia, NC and out of respect she sent a certified letter with documented medical proof form the doctor stating:

'*This is a medical necessity, that he take a DNA test in order to properly diagnose my disease of M.S.*' There by giving my father a chance to do just the right thing. Submit a DNA test. If you had a child who had a life threatening disease would you not do what you could to help him? If you had knowledge to know he was your child and had the power to help? If I had known my son had to have a bone marrow transplant for him to live, I would have done so but I didn't know. As we continue this story, the result of the letter, well first my father was given fifteen days to respond to the letter and I would supply the DNA test for him to submit, free of charge. The certified letter reached him January 27th 2017, he had until February 11th 2017 to reply or else I'd be prepared to file a court motion hoping that the judge would grant approval of forcing my father on medical basis to submit DNA.

Chapter 26

The Effects of The Opened Box

WHILE WAITING FOR the fifteen days to go by until the deadline for my father was up to submit the DNA or respond to the letter, I received a text from my brother, or should I say my father's son, which stated that I was no longer to contact my father or him and that all interactions would only be permitted through lawyers. Now I could not even verbally communicate with my father. What a pit that put in my stomach and a rip in my heart. Now on the sixteenth day I received a response back from the law firm representing my father, which is my brother's law firm in Detroit. The comment was, *'Your alleged father says he will not voluntarily submit his DNA in no circumstance under any condition.'* If I were to get a letter from my practicing physician stating exactly what medical questions needed to be answered then he would cooperate with that but no DNA. So in my mind that makes no logic. If you are not giving me DNA to prove that you are or that you are not my father then how would his medical information even be worthy of taking in consideration? There's no proof that he was my father. I know that once again I was at a wall but I knew that to get over this wall I would need a very high ladder or a crane to just knock it down. I text my brother and told him that I knew what he was trying to do. He was trying to throw me so far off my search and wear me down. That was not going to work, I would continue to fight and each time he'd block me off one path and put another wall up it would only make me more determined and more focused to what my purpose was. My purpose was to prove that he was my brother and that his father was my father. I also said this once again no longer a fact of feelings and emotions. It's a matter of pure desire and my principals to find the truth and that I will for all in my power to lay the path of truth right before him with no obstructions and obstacles. The path will be as clear as the runway of an airport and he will be cleared to land if he chooses.

On Thursday, February 16th, I received a call from a lawyer who was representing me. She stated to me, "As your attorney representing you, I wanted you to know that your father put an offer on the table." My heart sank in wonder could that finally be the miracle that I was looking for? I asked her what the offer was? I figured in my mind that would be that, he would take the DNA test but would want me to never again communicate with him in life. Or, that I would sign a consent for that would state that upon taking a DNA test that I would give all rights up to any family inheritance.

All these thoughts were racing through my mind as I was waiting for the attorney to just tell me what the offer was. Time froze and the lawyer said, "Your father says that he will submit to the DNA..." I was elated with joy but she continued with the craziest statement, "I never seen anything like this. Your father says he will submit his DNA to you for a price of $10,000!" I was crushed and so offended but all that I could do was laugh. Laugh because, really? What more could I expect from Pandora's box? The insanity must continue until the story ends and so the battle continues.

I am fully able to fully understand that the man who is supposed to be my father just raped me again of the love that I was searching for. So even though this hurts deep down I knew that the odds were so high against me but still I have DNA on my side because I am registered on many DNA sites. I have come as close as a second cousin so my search continues. I knew that he was my father and I would prove this. I was fighting for my identity again. I knew one thing for sure was that Jehovah had my back and that I was a very determined individual. I would not have reached my goal of finding my mother and sisters and family if I didn't persist against all odds. Not only did I believe in God and that his reach is never short, but I believed in myself. I was in this to win it because right then I had not only opened Pandora's box but I was standing in the middle of the box and the effects of that box were all around me. Even in the air that I breathed. I had to make sure that while I battle Pandora and my father and brother I didn't lose focus on what had been accomplished. I found my mother, I found love of family, and have strained the love of my wife who I had and do love dearly. I know it's my duty to mend the tear in the relationship that I had caused. My search and my journey was well justified because I am still trying and determined to complete me!

I knew and I recognized that once again against many odds of actually having a satisfactory result outcome from all of that. I had that journey of trying to establish my rightful place in my father's house being that I was his first born. Somehow, my birth right of first born has been sold in front of my face. My mere existence in that family file is somehow being deleted. The search was turning out to be a virus. But I had to protect myself with a, so to speak, antivirus. The Plexiglas had come back into affect.

Chapter 27

Family Feud

THE FACT OF the situation when I really face the fact is that I have found unity with my mother and siblings but with my father and his children I am ostracized, rejected. They wish I never was and never will be but once again this is totally unacceptable to me. I am here and even though the love is not there, the lineage is. Mr. Moore is in fact my father. All this comes together as I have a father who for whatever reason totally denies me. Besides the fact that I have just learned that my mother and father's wife were both pregnant at the same time. I am the oldest then a few months later came my sister from my father and his wife.

I also know that my brother who is the lawyer in Detroit, Moore law firm is my father's representative so here we go again. It's now my brother and father and his daughters against me. They just want me to go away, fall out of existence. They want me deleted. I am very grateful to the lawyer from North Carolina for her help and sincerity in assistance in helping me get this close. She gave me a lot of needed guidance and discernment and professional opinions of the whole case. She state that obviously I was the man's son but they were trying to hide something. I did everything that I could to make it absolutely no effort to submit DNA. I even brought the DNA kit to minimize the cost and I offered to bring the kit to Mr. Moore house(my father), so that he could submit it. She wrote my father a letter enclosing a letter from my mom stating that without a doubt that Mr. Moore was my biological father.

The Attorney enclosed in that letter dated February 1st 2017, Medical documentation from my treatment doctor that it was imperative to learn my biological roots to pinpoint my disease and the response that he would not voluntarily submit DNA. The Attorneys professional opinion to me was that I was ninety nine point nine percent his son. Mr. Moore knew this and so did his family and he even stated that on the Ancestry DNA that I had been conversing with his niece, which proves without a doubt that I was his son, because DNA does not lie!

"I know you are the person that is looking for the one percent, Mr. Jones. You have done a diligent search and in my opinion once again all parties involved in this know that without a shadow of doubt you are their family." She continued, "It's just that they for whatever reason want to accept you into their circle." I thought a lot about these words of truth and she is absolutely correct.

On February 17th 2017, I received a letter from the attorney who was nice enough to represent me for a small fee. In that letter to me the attorney said how nice it was to work with me, trying to get my father to submit the DNA but that she informed me that my father was willing to submit this DNA for a sum of ($10,000) ten thousand dollars. From this time on if I wished to retain her but her fee was a hundred and fifty dollars an hour. Although, I wish I could retain her this was and is beyond my pocket and so we parted. Before sent back all my documents she wrote me two letters of advice and one stated that she acknowledge that my father had offered to take the DNA for a fee of ten thousand dollars and that offer remained outstanding and that upon termination of our agreement that this leaves it open for my brother, who is my father's attorney, to work directly with me on this contract.

No more than one day later, my brother calls me and ask, "How do you want to proceed?"

"Send me the contract written that you agree to give me my father's DNA for exchange of $10,000, since this was your offer." I replied. He responded back saying that I was to put the ten thousand in escrow and that he would turn it around. I told him, "If you made an offer, agreement, or contract, then no one in their right mind is going to send anyone $10,000 without the terms of the contract written."

"I am not going to waste my time on writing anything because obviously you don't have the money and unless a judge orders my father to take the DNA test then it's simply not going to happen. If he does order it then I will appeal it and if I have to I will take this to the Supreme Court. This will never stop, never. You are not my brother, because my brother would not act in such a way." He stated. Then he went to say that I directly violated his mother and that I owe her a direct apology and maybe then and only then when I apologize to her I would get a pass. At that moment I felt that now this has become more bitter than a divorce case. My issue was never with him but with my father. So for now I had to cut all ties of communication with him.

The last words that he has sent me is that if this goes to the Supreme Court he would foot the bill. So in my mind that is exactly where I would like to take this. If he wants to go there then that's my goal in the first place. It wouldn't be any cost to me, that's perfect. In the next book, if possible, I will let you know if how this all turns out in the end or if I find out anything new before I finish writing then I will let you know. As stated before this is between my father and I. I have other options on the table in which I have taken an interest in and one is a private investigator who will get DNA and then I can submit it to a private lab. For now, I am going to work on other options and see what's all available that perhaps is at my disposal. The purpose of me writing this part of my journey is so that all readers can fully understand that when you are searching for your biological mother or father there are many feelings that come. That every fraction of the facts will forever alter the lives and affect all parties involved. You have to be willing to sacrifice the very thing that you are looking to find in order to achieve your goal. You are not always going to find acceptance. Just because you want to be accepted and because you want to find your family, does not mean that your family wants to be found.

Chapter 28

My Mom

IN MY SEARCH for my mother there was a lesson that I learned. Simply put is that there is a vast difference between a dad and a father or a sperm donor. Most of all there's a difference between a mother and a mom. I say that because a mother is a role that the woman who gave birth to you plays as part of her responsibility to bring you into this world. For some it's the same as a job, feed, clothe, and educate your child. Some mother's abandon their position, some by choice and some by circumstance. Then there is the mom and the mom not only provides but she nurtures and loves, cares, and gives you affection. A mom not only gives you direction but disciplines you so later in life, hopefully you remember and don't make mistakes that can cause harm or devastation to you. A mom you can confide in and a mom gets to know the personalities of her children. A mom is a protector.

I was looking for my mother but I can truly say that I found my mom and I can feel her love. One day I asked my mom, "Ma, if you had to give a description of me today what would it be?"

My mom paused and replied, "Boy, I know you love to talk that's one thing but I know for a fact that you love me." Then she paused and said, "I know you love me because mommy can feel your love." Those were the simplest but greatest words of all my fifty four years of living. For this is what I searched for is my mother and my mother's maternal love. So my mission had been accomplished as strange as it might sound after all those years fighting my mom's love. When I met my mom on the first day in which I was a nervous wreck I still had my emotions so far pushed down that I felt such a distance. I was still in the Plexiglas protective mode. It took a while to rip down that protective barrier. Even though I was relieved and so forever grateful to have my mom in my arms, it seemed as if that was only a dream. It actually took a few weeks for reality to set in. That I found my lifeline.

I was so used to fighting and hearing no that when I got the ultimate *'YES, you're my son'* and my first embrace, that I was actually terrified that the fight was over. Now I had to learn a new behavior called love. I had stuffed it down for so many years and at the same time I now had family all in one day. I had to now get rid of the miserable me. That miserable me is who I was comfortable with that's who I was and what I knew. I, now, have found my mother. Everything that I could wish for as far as human qualities are involved.

I am grateful to have found my mother still in the land of the living but of course wish that I had my whole lifetime to have gotten to know her. I try my best to make everyday count as if I knew my mom a lifetime. I love my mom like any son should and she loves me as any mom should. Somehow it seems like a black hole or vortex as strange as it sounds. It seems as if I have known my mom for my entire life and I have the same bond with my sisters. It's a gift but yet a strange occurrence. My life with my new family has seemed to be a continuation and not a new occurrence. It's like I had just went away for a couple of months and now I'm back Not that I had never existed in their lives and now here I am I have no complaints about it all. I am ecstatic to be accepted and I thank God everyday three or four times a day at a minimum.

Now my relationship with my mom is wonderful. I believe that our connection is a healing to both of us and I feel as I heal my mother heals. This is a two fold miracle. I know that in her heart she can't believe that I found her after fifty four years but she is ecstatic. My mom is not a very emotional person as far as I have observed but neither have I been. I believe a lot of that was from me being away from her since she was the age of sixteen. As a mom you have to feel each and every year on my birthdate my mom had to wonder how is her son, how does he look? Where he lives and what kind of person is he?

My mother had to have had a void in her heart. Even though she had other children, I was the one that was not there for her to have and care for and now I am here and no one has to tell me but I know for a fact that I hold a special part in my mom's heart. I fought the world to find my mother and so without a doubt I earned my rights to her heart and at the same time now this hurt for her can be done with and she can heal and smile. My mother can go to her grave satisfied and with a smile. All of her children are together.

In the same breath I am starting to heal and smile. My physical health is improving and my mental state of mind is changing. I can finally take off my military fatigue and live the civilian life. I have come home the fight is over. So together we grow, me and mama. Together we love me and mama, together we laugh, together we smile. Together we cry. I help her and she helps me. I give her strength and she gave me life. Our relationship is as best friends at the same time I have to remember that this is my mom. Sometimes I talk to my mother and after I have let her know some personal aspects of my life then I think should I have said that? But how else is my mother going to know me if I don't be honest with her and talk to her? Our conversations are mutual, we have so much in common and I finally have someone that I can talk to who seem to understand my wave link of rationality. Sometimes I'll ask my mother to explain back to me what I have tried to explain to her and she was never off. She always said, "Boy, I know exactly what you were saying!" Then she would break it down to me and to my surprise, she had been right on each time. Sometimes in life it seems that no one could understand my explanation of how I perceive life and how I see the world. It's been that way for many years so in reality I stop trying to reason with people to try to make them understand my angle of my perception in life. When I talk to my mom it no big thing just as if it were everyday conversation. It is so good to be able to communicate with someone on your level of understanding. I am so grateful to have my mother in my life and have such a good and close relationship with her. I am glad that we are healing each other. I am glad not only to have my mother in my life but I am the happiest son in the world to have my mom. My healing could only come from God and my mom and her healing is the same from God and her son. Because if I didn't find her and fight for my rights I would still be miserable and if she didn't open her heart to me then my mom would still be incomplete.

Once again a big part of who I am is from my parents Theodore and Mildred Jones and the choice that I was given to them enabled me to be the man that I am today. I am in reality lucky to have had two mothers and two moms in my lifetime. Maybe as a needy child I knew what is in God's hand and His purpose. I am so very happy to have made it through this emotional struggle. Surely when I could no longer walk on my own, Jehovah carried me through. All praises go to Him for giving me the courage and wisdom and understanding to take on the impossible. The strength and fortitude to carry on and reach the mountaintop. My mom and I have a special soul connection. When I talk to my mom it's like it just me and her. A straight life connection to the umbilical cord. Private access, VIP, backstage. My mom and I have so much in common even down to what foods and snacks we enjoy. The endless talks about things and the way is was in New York. I think how crazy it was to have found my mom and how I realized that yes, I had a portion of love but there indeed is no love like a mother's love.

Each and everyday I draw strength and wisdom and love from my mother. I am getting stronger and stronger as I absorb and take her very being into me. It is as if a transfer of her soul to me so that she will always continue to have a legacy through me. I am still a gatekeeper but my past is no longer vulnerable and sad. My responsibility at this gate is now of a watch of enlightenment and joy. Behind my gate is family, hope, love, care, happiness, wisdom, and light.

Chapter 29

Effects of Adoption

I ASSUME THAT by me writing my story and letting you into my mind uninhibited, you have to see the facts as they were and as they are. As I am sure you might not understand my mindset meaning the way I perceive and see the world or how situations have affected the trend of my thought. There are those of you that are right there where I was. There are those who just don't have the nerve to turn yourselves inside out in order to expose the inner you to the outside world in fear to face the facts or stigma that is always attached to the unknown or misunderstood. So here I have done this for you so in essence if you think no one could understand your pain, your frustration, your fears, your thoughts, or your story, I am here to assure you that I do. You are not alone. Yes you will feel isolated as an individual but the fact is you are not alone. So speak up even though you might seem alone.

There are millions that are going through what you are going through exactly and the effects of adoption affect millions more as it affects families involved, brothers, sisters, mothers, fathers, etc. For some the journey is grateful and fulfilling and the end result are joyful and they receive the embrace of love and family. For others the journey is unfulfilling gray, dark, hard, and treacherous and the person searching for their loved ones and family become hated and disowned and end up being a living hell. I feel qualified to express these thoughts to you because in my search I have experiences both. Heaven in the search for my mom and sisters and brother and then hell in the search for my father. I am grateful still to be on Earth and here to pass on my experience, strength, and hope to all those in the midst of the battle to find their families and themselves. One thing I learned in my search is about myself and I found myself I built up myself worth by subtracting all negativity out of my own equation. You too will learn what you are made of as you face the many obstacles to find your family. You will discover your strengths and you will be constantly looking at that imaginary mirror which at the end of the day that imaginary mirror will transition to virtual mirror which in turn will be transformed in to your physical image of you. So don't be surprised that at the end of the day that you find a new you, a happy you. Stay positive even when things look impossible, stay positive when all the facts look negative. Stay up when all things look low go high when they go low. Take time to think, don't lose your focus. When the world seems to be spinning around you don't get dizzy keep your eye on your goal. If you get too dizzy and lost.... Get off the merry go round and get your self together. Don't forget where you left off at, or get side track always return back to the purpose, Remember why you are on your journey and what you are determined to accomplish.

If you vow to find yourself, then how can you give up on yourself? Stay focused at all times no matter how many distractions surround you don't give up on yourself. If you are truly focused on your destination then let it be your goal to reach that destination. Your journey of finding you and your family starts with you and at the end of the day ends with you. Only you live in your mind, you can share your thoughts with others but your own thoughts are exactly what they are, your thoughts. At the end of the day you have to deal with those thoughts and sort those thoughts out your emotions and feelings are all yours and so are your accomplishments. It's all apart of who you are and your physical make up. So like a fine tuned watch every mechanism must work as one unit in proper sequence to accomplish it's purpose. The watch too, precisely tells time and your body's mechanisms, thoughts, feelings, and emotions, to properly fulfill your journey.

The one body mechanism that I could not seem to keep in check was the stress and anxiety level. There were days and I might even say months where I could feel my heart beating in my temples as though my brain was my heart itself. It seemed as if my head would expand and then would contract. In my brain at times I could hear the blood flowing with stress in my brain as if my head was the beach and the water was rushing back and forth to the shore and then receding back into the ocean. Constantly pulling the sands of sanity away from the only foundation that I had, my mind. The stress level had been so bad that there was an increased amount of pain in my head. I felt blood vessels in my brain expand to the point of capacity as if someone cut off the supply of blood to certain vessels in my brain and caused them to have the same reaction as a man made dam would. All my blood was confined and held back at the same time my brain could not get the right amount of oxygen to survive in order to make my brain function. But through this I had to dig down deeper that I ever had to dig into myself to find the inner strength within the inner strength. The last blood drops of my existence in order to grind through my misery and darkness where it was literally my mind against my body. My pure desire against my brain. I knew it was to death do us part. I was married and self dedicated to finding the truth of who I was. My journey to an extended cleansing was the only reason I ate is because I knew I had to function. My body needed food to survive and that was primarily the reason that I ate was to survive to accomplish my purpose.

All things are possible. I have found thriving life under the graves. Jehovah is great. All respect and praise truly goes to God for this remarkable blessing of my family. Also to have a wife that stood by me as I entered and lived in Hell's Gate. I walked in as a possessed evil spirit a heavily weighed down desparate destitute miserable cold uncaring suicidal soul, heavy spirited enslaved in my own misery and self inflicted torment of my own damnation. In misery and pain of unbearable persecution of my very being. Even the air that I inhaled was of substantial weight. The air that I gasped for to survive was actually me breathing in my own bloo suffocating on my own very source of life. My body was only a shell surviving with a heart that had no beat a body with out a pulse. My thoughts were different than my mind. My very thoughts were clotted with maggots of pain and despair eating at the very last fibers of my sanity these maggots of my mind had infested and infected the very being of who I was as a living Human. The blood that flowed through my veins were clotted and three times the consistency. My soul was weighed down from the crown of my head to the soles of my feet.

But with God's help, I flew out of Hell's Gates with wings, light and unweighed. I soared amongst the eagles and hawks as I looked down at the bubbling lava of Hell Through my eyes from a great distance while catching the pockets of fresh air gliding amongst the clouds and blue skies and felt the warmth of sun. As I glided through freedom no longer feeling the unbearable effects of the three hundred and sixty degrees of stress and Hell. How great it was to be able to breath and not feel like I am forever drowning in my own miserable fate. Free at last, free at last... thank God almighty free at last. I have truly reached the mountain top. Now, I could float and swim not a journey to the bottom with a weight attached to my neck, going deeper and deeper and deeper, spiraling out of control to my doom. Now I traveled up, I glided, I soared. I, at the age of fifty four was born again. Even though I was in the land of the living. I started living all over again from what I missed for fifty four years. Just really think about it, (really enter my mind): I have been searching for my family since I was five years old. Now that I have found my mother, I am trying to get whatever information of my life that I missed from her. Like what meals she cooked? What was life like in the house if I had have been with five sisters and a brother? What kind of relationship would I have had with my mother? Would my father be in my life now? What kind of person would I have been today if I had been brought up in my mother's house? What place would I have in my mother's heart and what place do I have now?

At the same time, I am so grateful that I have my mother in my life. This struggle was over and I've gotten the chance now to get to know her. Although, I know that my father is not accepting me, I know that my mom loves me and that's what ninety nine percent of the war and journey was about. Now before I forget, I have to get back to my father for a moment. During my research for Mr. Moore, there were addresses that came up as locations that my father resided. One address that came up was Wyndover Woods. This will of course sound so shocking but I lived on Lincoln and South Road, Wyndover Woods was and still is on South Road, which is exactly one block up the street from where I grew up.

I stood right at the bus stop for over ten years right across the street from Wyndover Woods apartments., from elementary school to high school. My bus stop was in front of my biological father's house, one of my friends lived in that very building which was a four apartment dwelling. I would frequently go to my friend's apartment that lived in the same building as my father. As a child, in the winter I would sleigh right there next to One Wyndover Woods for hours! When I got older and had a family dog, that was where the designated area where my dog would love to run and go to the bathroom. As I child I would pass my father's house to get to the park to play ball or just hang out.

Just figured that you might find this aspect very puzzling because to this day, I wonder if my adopted parents or my biological father had any knowledge of this coincidence? I guess stranger things have happened. Maybe one day I'll get to answer that question: if either knew of the other? Those questions will come in time and earlier in the chapter I told you I would keep you posted if any new information arrives on the search for my father.

So with that to say I lost more than twenty- five pounds from years of this stress. Pretty much my body was living off of whatever muscles and fat that my body had stored. So yes it's all a fine balance but once again I am on the rebound and will continue to get stronger especially my mind. Here I am actually able to speak and verbalize what was and is going on inside of me in order to help others to feel and recognize what they are going through. Once again writing this book had a certain healing property for me. I gave it to the world and personally to you because there is no shame but these have merely been the facts and I wanted to truly thank each and every person who is reading this book. Thanks for taking the time to get to know me, Preston, as I have brought you into my mind, through the power of sight, smell, touch, and sound. Now I leave you with who I am and what I have discovered about myself, now what about you? Anything is possible if only you believe. If only you believe the impossible is possible. Now you can close your minds on my journey and start your own but please.. please dont forget my journey as you embark on your own journey It is my hope that through the insight of my journey you will be able to gain the strength and fortitude to conquer whatever obstacles fall in your path. But please pass my story on... Remember these are just the facts and only the facts, do with them as you will. Thank you for coming into my world and my mind. May your dreams become a reality as have mine. Much love to you... MAY THE FORCE BE WITH YOU...... LIVE LONG AND PROSPER!!!!!!

> The mountains are my bones
> The rivers are my veins
> The forest are my thoughts
> And the stars are my dreams
> The ocean is my heart, it's pounding in my poise
> The songs of the earth write the music
> To my soul.

> -Kiera Nicole

Acknowledgements

I WANT TO thank the many people through thoughts and who listened tireless to me as I told them of my ambition to find my mother. I thank them for their special input and most of all their listening ear and words of encouragement. As I put this crazy fantasy of finding my mother to a reality and a success.

- I thank God, Jehovah, for listening to my prayers and giving me the strength to carry on when it was inhumanly impossible for me.
- I thank my wife, Lisa for putting up with my misery for the last eight years as I struggled and ripped all my love and emotions from our relationship and denied her of my love. As well as mental support as I totally too me out of our relationship in order to find myself. Thank you Lisa for your preservation.
- Thank you Big Tim, Timothy Williams, Squeeze, for the mental support and the technical support. The setup of my Facebook and the brotherly ear and love given and for taken this battle with me personally side by side as a soldier, a friend, a brother, my back. Thank you for countless heartfelt dedication even in sickness you put my search first. You were a real trooper Tim and I'll miss you Bro. See you in Paradise, you fought well my brother.
- Auntie Cherry Griffin, thanks for the many hours, day in and day out for the wisdom and advice and encouragement.
- James Vernon Marable, best friend and father figure. Thanks for the big heart and support and shoulder to lean on and

when no one else was there you were tears and heart. When no one else believe, you believed. When there was no one to give the leftover, overwhelming pain, you took it through the thick and thin. You stayed regardless of the consequences or what anyone else thought. Vernon you were there and still is. I learned character from you and learned that you are a true friend. Thank you Vernon Marable. If there were more people like you the world would be a better place.

- Mother in Law, Sheila Guzman (Mom), very seldom do son in laws get along with their mother in laws. But mom got right in there with me, through her sickness. She got on the phone and called and found the first person with the name Snell, which kept me searching. Mom spent countless hours tracking and recording the Snell family line. Excellent secretarial skills. Mom was my personal psychologist, my stress reliever. She endured a lot in life as the caretaker and being the caretaker she gave it to me raw and uncut and is the person of great insight and wisdom. Thank you for being just who you are.

- James Scurry for being a friend through all this craziness. Thanks for the support and continuous friendship and willingness to go the extra mile. There are few people in my life that I can label as a friend but there are fewer that are true friends and that's exactly what you are. Thanks James for the love and support and wisdom.

- Joyce Evans has been a great, great, mental support to me and was there from the beginning helping to be my ears and eyes in New York. Joyce made the medical connections for my doctors in New York, arranged my MRI's, and my MS appointments in New York. Because of the introduction to the right doctor, my case for my adoption was unsealed. I am forever grateful to you Joyce for the care, love, and consideration in all that you're done.

- Mom. Mildred Elizabeth Jones. Thank you mom for adopting me and giving me the best life that you could. Thank you for caring for me and giving me all that you had. I thank you for providing me with guidance and spiritual training. Thank you for caring for me when I was sick. Thank you mom for your time and your hugs. Thank you for loving me and caring for me as your own son. I love you mom and will always love you. Wishing that you were still alive but your love and smile are always alive in my heart. See you in paradise.

- Thank you Tion Dudley (my nephew) for my cover art.
- Ronnie Brantley for the tech support and videography
- My niece- Timia Williams for the editing, proofing, and grammar support.
- Thanks to my Baby sister Bridgette for being a second eye and ear in the final editing.
- Thank you to all whose names I did not list that had a part in helping me accomplish my dream.

Ending Poem by Preston

In the night I toss and turn
Inside my body it seems my mind starts to burn.
I think 'wow' Jehovah's approval
my mom truly earned.
My pain so deep for now I very rarely sleep.
Then calmness comes over my soul,
And I think, mu mom passed at 77 years old.
A fine fight always having Jehovah's will in sight,
Mom you were the best… That's a secret
that can't be kept.
Mom I miss your hugs and your kisses.
But, surely now you have accomplished your deepest
wishes – (a ticket to paradise) where the lion
and the lamb feed and lie as one.
No More death and sorrow, peace and love form grand
creator Jehovah above.

I pray that I make it to the new system.
Where I will wait and patiently listen on Jehovah to say:
Mildred come on out, you are now free from the grips
of the death and hades…here you come from the grave,
a beautiful young vibrant lady.

Mom – See you in Paradise

Family Photos

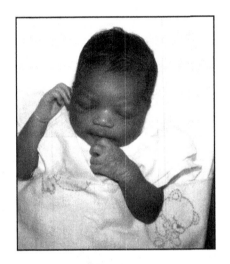

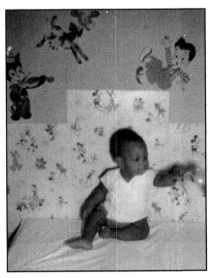

My adoptive parents.

This is the actual house where I grew up.

BIG TIM

Me besides Mom, 8-5 years old.

Links and Newspaper Articles

Links

Http://youtu.be/7xCFRp_90Z4 "Man Meets His Mother For First Time"

- "Where are you Mommy?" YouTube 19:32- January 22, 2015, Preston Jones
- "I found you Mommy!" YouTube 4:51- August 5, 2015 Preston Jones

Newspaper Articles

Virginian-Pilot Tuesday, August 18, 2015

Pilotonline.com, Story by Elizabeth Simpson, 'Searching for Mom', August 18, 2015

Greensboro N.C. Newspaper, Teresa Prout, 'You Are Here Now' Greensboro.com, Sunday, August 30, 2015

Email:
PrestonJones10@cox.net
Or
Facebook Preston Jones

On September 23, 2017, I actually met my father
face to face so now I am complete as a person.

Printed in the United States
By Bookmasters